The Cocktail

The
Cocktail

over 200 classic and contemporary cocktails

Bath · New York · Singapore · Hong Kong · Cologne · Delhi · Melbourne

First published by Parragon in 2010

Parragon Publishing
Queen Street House
4 Queen Street
Bath BA1 1HE, UK

ISBN: 978-1-4075-5372-6

Printed in China

Introduction by Dominic Utton
Illustrations by Kristel Steenbergen
Cover design by Andrew Easton @ Ummagumma
Internal design by Sabine Vonderstein

Notes for the Reader
This book uses imperial, metric, and U.S. cup measurements. Follow the same units
of measurement throughout; do not mix imperial and metric. All spoon measurements
are level: teaspoons are assumed to be 5 ml, tablespoons are assumed to be 15 ml,
and one measure is assumed to be 1½ oz. Unless otherwise stated, milk is assumed
to be whole and eggs are medium-size. Recipes using raw eggs should be avoided
by the elderly, pregnant women, convalescents, and anyone with a chronic condition.
Please consume alcohol responsibly.

CONTENTS

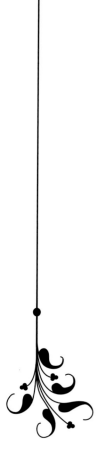

INTRODUCTION

ALTHOUGH IT'S REASONABLE TO ASSUME THAT COCKTAILS ARE A MODERN INVENTION, THEY HAVE IN FACT BEEN AROUND FOR ABOUT AS LONG AS PEOPLE HAVE BEEN DRINKING, AS BARMEN TRIED DIFFERENT COMBINATIONS OF SPIRITS TO SUIT DIFFERENT TASTES.

However, it wasn't until 1806 that they acquired a formal definition, when New York publication *The Balance* declared: "A cocktail is a stimulating liquor composed of spirits of any kind, sugar, water, and bitters... it renders the heart stout and bold, at the same time that it fuddles the head."

It took another 56 years before budding "mixologists" were given clear recipes. The 1862 book *How to Mix Drinks or The Bon Vivant's Companion* by "Professor" Jerry Thomas contained guides to creating 10 drinks referred to as "cocktails"—including the first recipes for the Brandy Daisy and the Sour—forerunner of the Kamikaze, Sidecar, and Daiquiri. Thomas was also the first celebrity barman, famous for his flashy mixing technique. While in San Francisco he created the Blue Blazer, in which whiskey is set on fire and passed between two mixing glasses to create an arc of flame. As head bartender of the Occidental Hotel he earned $100 a week—more than the Vice President of the United States!

By the 1900s, cocktails had become the most fashionable drink in United States—a reputation cemented in May 1917, when Mrs. Julia S. Walsh Junior, of St. Louis, Missouri, invited 50 high-society guests to her house for drinks before lunch. "The party scored an instant hit," the local newspaper declared. "Within a matter of weeks, cocktail parties became a St. Louis institution."

Eight years later, English novelist Alec Waugh (brother of *Brideshead Revisited* author Evelyn) hosted the first British cocktail party, when he served rum swizzles to astonished guests who thought they had come for high tea.

By then, however, American drinkers were officially denied their favorite tipples under the laws of Prohibition, although far from suppressing consumption, the ban simply meant a growth in new and more interesting ways to mix drinks.

After the end of Prohibition in 1934, cocktails once again enjoyed a boom in popularity. New drinks, such as the Margarita, were invented, according to one account when Texan socialite Margarita Sames gave a party at which guests were invited to mix their own drinks. Her creation of three parts tequila, one part Triple Sec, and one part lime juice went down so well it quickly traveled from Texas to the rest of the country, bearing her name.

Cocktails continue to be invented today, often with wildly suggestive names and increasingly theatrical methods of preparation. Cocktail bars can be found in almost every major city in the world and all the best hotels pride themselves on their cocktail lists. Among barmen, competitions are held each year and awards given out to the world's best mixologists.

Cocktails are big business now, but nonetheless many of the basics from yesteryear still apply. A great cocktail is still a delicately balanced potion of strong, weak, sweet, and sour ingredients, delivered with a flourish and served perfectly chilled. And with just a few ingredients, a couple of items of specialist equipment, and the recipes in this book, it is possible to replicate any number of classic and contemporary cocktails in your own home.

Essential Equipment

Cocktail shaker
The standard type is a cylindrical metal container with a capacity of 2¼ cups that has a double lid incorporating a perforated strainer. If your cocktail shaker doesn't have an integral strainer, you will need a separate one.

Mixing glass
This is used for making stirred cocktails. You can use any large container or pitcher, but professional mixing glasses are also available.

Strainer
A bar strainer or Hawthorn strainer is the perfect tool to prevent ice and other unwanted ingredients from being poured from the shaker or mixing glass into the serving glass. If you don't have one, you could use a small nylon strainer instead.

Jigger
Also called a measure, this small measuring cup is often double-ended and shaped like an hourglass. Standard American jiggers are 1½ fl oz, representing 1 measure. The proportions of the various ingredients, but not the specific quantities, are critical, so if you don't have a jigger, you can use the small lid of your cocktail shaker, a shot glass, or even a small egg cup.

Bar spoon
This long-handled spoon is used for stirring cocktails in a mixing glass.

Muddler
This is simply a miniature masher used for crushing ingredients, such as herbs and sugar, in the base of a glass. You can also use a mortar and pestle or even the back of a spoon.

Other equipment
Lots of ordinary kitchen equipment is useful for making cocktails: A corkscrew, a bottle opener, toothpicks, a citrus reamer, cutting boards, knives, a citrus zester, a selection of pitchers, and a blender for creamy cocktails and slushes. You will also need an ice bucket and ice tongs—never pick up ice with your fingers. Optional extras include swizzle sticks and straws.

GLASSES

COCKTAIL OR MARTINI GLASS

The most immediately recognizable cocktail glass, the shape of the conical Martini glass helps to stop the ingredients from separating, while the stem keeps the drink cool.

COUPETTE GLASS

This glass is based on the earlier champagne coupe, originally used for serving bubbly. The wide bowl is perfect for rimming with salt, making it the ideal vessel for Margaritas.

HURRICANE GLASS

The shape of this large, short-stemmed glass is said to resemble the hurricane lamp, from which it gets its name. It was originally used for the famous Hurricane cocktail at New Orleans bar Pat O'Brien's, but is today associated with exotic frozen and blended cocktails.

CHAMPAGNE FLUTE

The tapered shape of this tall, thin glass is designed to reduce the liquid's surface area, thus keeping champagne bubbly for longer.

HIGHBALL GLASS

Highball glasses are tall and so suitable for simple drinks with a high proportion of mixer to spirit. They are versatile enough to be substituted for the similarly shaped, but slightly larger, Collins glass.

LOWBALL GLASS

The terms "lowball," "rocks," and "old-fashioned" are often used to refer to short, squat tumblers. They are perfect for holding ice and any spirit "on the rocks" and are also popular for short mixed drinks.

SHOT GLASS

A home-bar essential, the shot glass holds just enough liquid to be downed in one mouthful. It has a thick base to withstand being slammed on the bar.

IRISH COFFEE GLASS

The key features of an Irish coffee glass are that it's made of heatproof glass and it has a handle, which make it suitable for hot cocktails, such as toddies.

ESSENTIAL TECHNIQUES

CHILLING

For absolute perfection, you should chill spirits, mixers, and serving glasses in the refrigerator. However, it's not always possible to find room for glasses and you should never put fine crystal in the refrigerator. As an alternative, fill glasses with cracked ice and stir well, then tip out the ice and any water before pouring in the cocktail.

LAYERING

To make a layered shooter or pousse-café, you generally need to pour the heaviest liquid into the glass first, working through to the lightest. However, the real trick is the technique—you should touch the top of the drink with a long-handled bar spoon and pour the liquid slowly over the back of it to disperse it across the top of the ingredients already in the glass. Always add the liqueurs or spirits in the order specified in the recipe.

MUDDLING

Muddling means to mash fruit or herbs to release their flavors and it's done with an implement called a muddler. The technique is to press down with a twisting action. Sometimes, a small amount of liquid will be added to facilitate muddling, but the majority is usually poured in later. Popular muddled drinks include Caipirinhas and Mojitos.

SHAKEN OR STIRRED?

Shaking is the most flamboyant method of making a cocktail. It is good for chilling drinks and diluting them to just the right degree. To make a shaken cocktail, put cracked ice in a cocktail shaker and pour the ingredients listed in the recipe over it. Close securely and shake vigorously for 10–20 seconds, until the outside of the shaker is coated with condensation. Remove the small lid and strain the cocktail into the appropriate glass.

Stirring is the purist's choice—it is the mixology method that aims to retain the strength of the spirit. To make a stirred cocktail, put cracked (never crushed) ice in a mixing glass and pour the ingredients listed in the recipe over it. Using a long-handled spoon, stir vigorously for 20 seconds and strain into the appropriate glass.

Making sugar syrup

Even superfine sugar often fails to dissolve completely in the brief time that the cocktail is shaken or stirred, so it is better to use sugar syrup or syrop de gomme when sweetening drinks. To make sugar syrup, put 4 tablespoons water and 4 tablespoons superfine sugar into a small pan and stir over low heat until the sugar has dissolved. Bring to a boil, then continue to boil, without stirring, for 1–2 minutes, then let cool. Store in a sterilized jar or bottle in the refrigerator for up to 2 months.

Frosting glasses

Glasses can be frosted with sugar, or fine or coarse salt in the case of the Margarita or Salty Dog. Simply rub the rim of the glass with a lemon or lime wedge, then dip the glass upside down into a shallow saucer of sugar or salt until the rim is evenly coated.

Cracking and crushing ice

Store ice in the freezer until just before use. Cracked ice is used in both shaken and stirred cocktails. To crack ice, put ice cubes in a strong plastic bag and hit it against an outside wall, or put the ice between clean dish towels on a sturdy counter and crush with a wooden mallet or rolling pin. Crushed ice is used in cocktails made in a blender. To crush ice, crack it as above but break it into much smaller pieces. Alternatively, you can use a blender to crack or crush ice, although you'll need one with a powerful motor.

BASE SPIRITS

Spirits are the soul of any cocktail. Whatever flavorings, fruit juices, sugars, and spices come later, it all begins with the spirit. Although most people think of "spirits" as meaning any alcoholic drink other than beer or wine, for the purist cocktail mixer, there are six base spirits to work from.

BRANDY

Far more diverse than just your ordinary after-dinner brandy, there are actually three distinct types. Grape brandy, produced by the distillation of fermented grapes, is the most commonly known and includes cognac, Armagnac, and brandy de Jerez. Fruit brandy is distilled from apples, plums, peaches, apricots, and so on, resulting in distinctly flavored spirits, such as Calvados (from Normandy), German Schnapps, and Kirsch, made from cherries. Finally, pomace brandy, made from the grape seeds, skins, and stems, results in strong, clear varieties, such as the Italian spirit grappa.

RUM

Distilled from molasses (or occasionally sugarcane juice), rum is traditionally associated with the Caribbean and South America, and many of the rum-based cocktails, such as the Mojito and Daiquiri, have their origins in this area.

Although there are several varieties of the spirit, most cocktails tend only to use the "light" rums, such as Bacardi and cachaça, and their mild flavor and sweet taste make them ideal as a base for other mixers.

GIN

Created from grain-distilled alcohol and flavored with juniper berry oil (or sometimes sloe berries), gin's origins lie back in the 17th century, when it was used by Dutch doctors to treat kidney disorders and infections. It proved to be so popular that it soon found a market away from medicine and quickly spread around the world. Its origins, however, remain with us in the phrase "Dutch courage." Gin is also extremely easy to produce. During the Prohibition era, many speakeasies distilled their own "bathtub gin," which resulted in a boom in the popularity of Martinis, among other cocktails.

TEQUILA

Perhaps the most regional spirit of them all, most of the world's tequila is produced in a small area in western Mexico surrounding the city which gives it its name. It is made from fermenting the local agave plant, often a long, labor-intensive activity—in many cases the agave is still harvested by hand.

The resulting clear, "silver" spirit can be up to 55 percent ABV and is mostly drunk straight by native Mexicans or "shot" with salt and lime. It is also the basis for many cocktails, including the classic Margarita and the Long Island Iced Tea.

Whiskey

Covering a multitude of varieties around the world, all whiskeys are distilled from fermented grain mash (including barley, rye, wheat, and corn) and most are then aged in wooden casks.

The name is a shortened version of the ancient Gaelic word *usquebaugh,* which translates as "aquae vitae" or "water of life." The first written record of its production is in an Irish text of 1405, in which a Chieftain's death is put down to "a surfeit of aquae vitae," although it is believed to have been distilled in Ireland as early as the 6th century.

There are dozens of different methods of production, but the most popular are Scotch (made with malted barley and aged in oak casks for at least three years and one day), Irish whiskey (similar to Scotch, although distilled three times instead of two), and bourbon (produced in the United States and made from corn grain and aged at least two years).

Vodka

Derived from the Russian and Polish words for water (*voda* and *woda* respectively), vodka began life as an East European medicine in the 14th century. Although it was rarely drunk outside Europe until the mid-20th century, it is now one of the world's most popular drinks—in 1975 sales in the United States even overtook those of bourbon.

Distilled from anything rich in starch and sugar, vodka can be made from corn, rye, wheat, potatoes, molasses—even in some cases from simply fermenting a solution of sugar and yeast. The resulting clear, odorless spirit can be drunk neat but also makes an excellent base for hundreds of cocktails.

CLASSIC

Martini

SERVES 1

FOR MANY, THIS IS THE ULTIMATE COCKTAIL. IT IS NAMED AFTER ITS INVENTOR, MARTINI DI ARMA DI TAGGIA, NOT THE FAMOUS BRAND OF VERMOUTH! THE PROPORTIONS OF THE SPIRITS IN A MARTINI CAN VARY HUGELY—THIS IS THE ORIGINAL VERSION.

3 measures gin
1 tsp dry vermouth, or to taste
cracked ice cubes
green cocktail olive, to decorate

1. Pour the gin and vermouth over cracked ice in a mixing glass and stir well to mix.
2. Strain into a chilled cocktail glass and dress with the cocktail olive.

THE LEGEND MARTINI

SERVES I

THIS FRUITY VERSION OF THE UBIQUITOUS MARTINI IS THE
STUFF OF WHICH LEGENDS — AT LEAST IN THE WORLD OF
COCKTAILS — ARE MADE.

2 measures vodka, iced
1 measure blackberry liqueur
1 measure lime juice
dash sugar syrup
cracked ice cubes

1. Shake all the ingredients
   vigorously over cracked ice
   until well frosted.
2. Strain into a chilled cocktail glass.

MARTINEZ

SERVES 1

2 measures gin, iced
1 measure Italian vermouth
dash Angostura bitters
dash maraschino liqueur
cracked ice cubes
lemon zest strip, to decorate

1. Shake the gin, vermouth, Angostura bitters, and maraschino liqueur over cracked ice until frosted.
2. Strain into a chilled cocktail glass and dress with the lemon zest.

MANHATTAN

SERVES 1

dash Angostura bitters
3 measures rye whiskey
1 measure sweet vermouth
cracked ice cubes
cocktail cherry, to decorate

1. Shake the liquids over cracked ice in a mixing glass and mix well.
2. Strain into a chilled cocktail glass and dress with the cocktail cherry.

WHISKEY SOUR

SERVES 1

1 measure lemon or lime juice
2 measures blended whiskey
1 tsp confectioners' sugar or sugar syrup
cracked ice cubes
lime slice and cocktail cherry, to decorate

1. Shake the lemon juice, whiskey, and sugar well over cracked ice.
2. Strain into a chilled cocktail glass and dress with the lime slice and cocktail cherry.

KAMIKAZE

SERVES 1

1 measure vodka
1 measure Triple Sec
½ measure lime juice
½ measure lemon juice
cracked ice cubes
dry white wine, chilled
cucumber slices, to decorate

1. Shake the vodka, Triple Sec, lime juice, and lemon juice together over cracked ice until well frosted.
2. Strain into a chilled glass and top off with wine.
3. Dress with the cucumber slices.

DAIQUIRI

SERVES 1

DAIQUIRI IS A TOWN IN CUBA, WHERE THIS DRINK WAS SAID TO HAVE
BEEN INVENTED. A BUSINESSMAN HAD RUN OUT OF IMPORTED GIN
AND SO HAD TO MAKE DO WITH THE LOCAL DRINK—RUM—WHICH, AT
THAT TIME, WAS OFTEN OF UNRELIABLE QUALITY.

2 measures white rum
¾ measure lime juice
½ tsp sugar syrup
cracked ice cubes

1. Pour the rum, lime juice, and
   sugar syrup over cracked ice and
   shake vigorously until well frosted.
2. Strain into a chilled cocktail glass.

MARGARITA

SERVES 1

WIDELY ATTRIBUTED TO FRANCISCO MORALES AND INVENTED
IN 1942 IN MEXICO, THIS IS A MORE CIVILIZED VERSION OF THE
ORIGINAL WAY TO DRINK TEQUILA—LICK OF SALT FROM THE BACK OF
YOUR HAND, SUCK OF LIME JUICE, AND A SHOT OF TEQUILA!

lime wedges
coarse salt
cracked ice cubes
3 measures white tequila
1 measure Triple Sec or
   Cointreau
2 measures lime juice

1. Rub the rim of a chilled cocktail
   glass with a lime wedge, then dip
   in a saucer of coarse salt to frost.
2. Put the cracked ice into a cocktail
   shaker. Pour in the tequila, Triple
   Sec, and lime juice and shake
   vigorously until well frosted.
3. Strain into the glass and dress
   with a lime wedge.

THE ERA OF PROHIBITION

JANUARY 16, 1920 SHOULD HAVE BEEN A DARK DAY
FOR AMERICAN COCKTAIL LOVERS. THE 18TH AMENDMENT TO
THE U.S. CONSTITUTION, ALSO KNOWN AS THE NATIONAL PROHIBITION
ACT, MADE "THE MANUFACTURE, SALE, OR TRANSPORTATION OF
INTOXICATING LIQUORS" ILLEGAL. AS IT TURNED OUT, IT BECAME
THE START OF A WHOLE NEW ERA OF GLAMOUR AND INNOVATION
FOR THE COCKTAIL.

The public was not going to give up drinking that easily and, with
no legal bars or clubs to share a tipple in, "speakeasies"—so named
because patrons could "speak easily" about alcohol without fear of the
authorities listening in—opened in their hundreds of thousands across
the nation. Speakeasies were by definition illegal and they were almost
inevitably run by gangsters, bootlegging alcohol from Canada, Mexico,
and the Caribbean or else making their own moonshine for sale.

The government simply could not control every border and nor could
they shut down every new illegal club that sprang up. By 1925, there
were an estimated 100,000 in New York alone, and in Chicago the
gangster Al Capone built up a criminal empire on the back of his
10,000 speakeasies in the city and ruled the bootlegging business from
Canada to Florida.

These were places where a man could enjoy a drink, but they were
also given a glamour and cachet by Prohibition itself. Drinking in a
speakeasy meant soaking up a little of that Mafioso mystique and so
people accordingly didn't simply stick to a bottle of beer, a glass of
wine, or even a shot of whiskey. If you were going to break the law,
you broke it in style—you ordered yourself a cocktail.

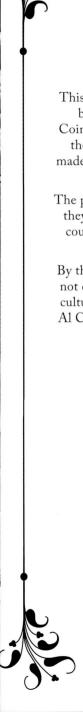

This was the "Roaring Twenties" and, despite Prohibition, cocktails had never been so popular. The Sidecar—a French concoction made with cognac, Cointreau, and lemon juice—became the defining drink of the era, along with the Whiskey Old Fashioned, and for the wealthier patrons the French 75, made with London gin and French champagne and named after a hard-hitting World War I artillery piece, was a must for any gentleman drinker.

The popularity of cocktails during Prohibition was in part down to the glamour they gave the drinker but it was also due to necessity—a well-mixed cocktail could disguise the less-than-perfect quality of some of the knock-off hooch smuggled in by the bootleggers.

By the early 1930s, the American government finally caved in. Prohibition had not curbed alcohol consumption—if anything it had created a whole drinking culture in itself, as well as providing a lucrative black market for mobsters like Al Capone. In 1933, the 18th amendment was officially repealed and cocktails were once again both fashionable and legal.

MINT JULEP

SERVES 1

leaves from 1 fresh mint sprig,
    plus an extra sprig to decorate
1 tbsp sugar syrup
crushed ice cubes
3 measures bourbon whiskey

1. Put the mint leaves and sugar syrup into a small chilled glass and mash with a muddler or spoon.
2. Add the crushed ice and stir to mix before adding the bourbon.
3. Dress with the mint sprig.

MOSCOW MULE

SERVES 1

2 measures vodka
1 measure lime juice
cracked ice cubes
ginger beer
lime slice, to decorate

1. Shake the vodka and lime juice vigorously over cracked ice until well frosted.
2. Fill a chilled tall glass halfway with cracked ice and strain over the cocktail.
3. Top off with ginger beer. Dress with the lime slice.

Salty Dog

Serves 1

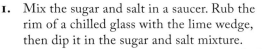

1 tbsp granulated sugar
1 tbsp coarse salt
lime wedge
cracked ice cubes
2 measures vodka
grapefruit juice

1. Mix the sugar and salt in a saucer. Rub the rim of a chilled glass with the lime wedge, then dip it in the sugar and salt mixture.
2. Fill the prepared glass halfway with cracked ice and pour over the vodka.
3. Top off with grapefruit juice and stir to mix.

Rusty Nail

Serves 1

cracked ice cubes
1 measure Scotch whisky
1 measure Drambuie

1. Fill an old-fashioned glass halfway with cracked ice.
2. Pour in the whisky and Drambuie and stir well.

HURRICANE

SERVES 1

THIS FLAMBOYANT COCKTAIL IS SYNONYMOUS WITH PAT O'BRIEN'S BAR IN THE NEW ORLEANS' FRENCH QUARTER. IT WAS CREATED DURING WORLD WAR II WHEN LIQUOR, SUCH AS WHISKEY, WAS IN SHORT SUPPLY BUT RUM WAS PLENTIFUL.

cracked ice cubes
4 measures dark rum
1 measure lemon juice
2 measures orange and passion fruit juice
club soda
orange slices and cocktail cherries, to decorate

1. Fill a tall glass with cracked ice.
2. Shake the rum, lemon juice, and orange and passion fruit juice until well combined and pour into the glass.
3. Top off with club soda and dress with the orange slices and cocktail cherries.

Long Island Iced Tea

Serves 1

Dating back to the days of Prohibition when it was drunk out of cups in an attempt to fool the FBI, this cocktail has evolved from the original simple combination of vodka with a dash of cola!

cracked ice cubes
2 measures vodka
1 measure gin
1 measure white tequila
1 measure white rum
½ measure white crème
  de menthe
2 measures lemon juice
1 tsp sugar syrup
cola
lime wedge, to decorate

1 Fill a tall glass with cracked ice.
2. Shake the vodka, gin, tequila, rum, crème de menthe, lemon juice, and sugar syrup vigorously over cracked ice until well frosted.
3. Strain into the glass and top off with cola.
4. Dress with the lime wedge.

Gin Sling Cocktail

Serves 1

cracked ice cubes
juice ¾ lemon
½ tbsp confectioners' sugar
1 measure gin
still water
dash Angostura bitters
lemon slice, to decorate

1. Fill a lowball glass halfway with cracked ice. Stir in the lemon juice, sugar, and gin.
2. Top off with still water, then add the Angostura bitters. Dress with the lemon slice.

White Lady

Serves 1

2 measures gin
1 measure Triple Sec
1 measure lemon juice
cracked ice cubes

1. Shake the gin, Triple Sec, and lemon juice vigorously over cracked ice until well frosted.
2. Strain into a chilled cocktail glass.

CHARLESTON

SERVES 1

¼ measure gin
¼ measure dry vermouth
¼ measure sweet vermouth
¼ measure Cointreau
¼ measure Kirsch
¼ measure maraschino liqueur
cracked ice cubes
thinly pared lemon rind, to decorate

1. Shake all the liquid ingredients vigorously over cracked ice until well frosted.
2. Strain into a chilled cocktail glass and dress with the lemon rind.

LONDON FRENCH 75

SERVES 1

2 measures London gin
1 measure lemon juice
cracked ice cubes
champagne, chilled

1. Shake the gin and lemon juice vigorously over cracked ice until well frosted.
2. Strain into a chilled glass and top off with champagne.

ZOMBIE

SERVES I

THE INDIVIDUAL INGREDIENTS OF THIS COCKTAIL, INCLUDING THE
LIQUEURS AND FRUIT JUICES, VARY CONSIDERABLY FROM ONE RECIPE
TO ANOTHER, BUT ALL ZOMBIES CONTAIN A MIXTURE OF WHITE,
GOLDEN, AND DARK RUM.

2 measures dark rum
2 measures white rum
1 measure golden rum
1 measure Triple Sec
1 measure lime juice
1 measure orange juice
1 measure pineapple juice
1 measure guava juice
1 tbsp grenadine
1 tbsp orgeat syrup
1 tsp Pernod
crushed ice cubes
fresh mint sprigs and pineapple
   wedges, to decorate

1. Shake all the liquids together over crushed ice until well combined and frosted.
2. Pour, without straining, into a chilled glass.
3. Dress with the mint sprigs and pineapple wedges.

BLOODY MARY

SERVES I

THERE ARE NUMEROUS VERSIONS OF THIS CLASSIC COCKTAIL — SOME ARE MUCH HOTTER AND SPICIER THAN OTHERS. THE INGREDIENTS MAY INCLUDE HORSERADISH SAUCE IN ADDITION TO OR INSTEAD OF THE TABASCO SAUCE.

dash Worcestershire sauce
dash Tabasco sauce
cracked ice cubes
2 measures vodka
splash dry sherry
6 measures tomato juice
juice ½ lemon
pinch celery salt
pinch cayenne pepper
celery stalk and lemon slice, to
    decorate

1. Dash the Worcestershire sauce and Tabasco sauce over cracked ice in a cocktail shaker and add the vodka, dry sherry, tomato juice, and lemon juice.
2. Shake vigorously until frosted.
3. Strain into a chilled tall glass, add the celery salt and cayenne pepper, and dress with the celery stalk and lemon slice.

TOM COLLINS

SERVES 1

3 measures gin
2 measures lemon juice
½ measure sugar syrup
cracked ice cubes
club soda
lemon slice, to decorate

1. Shake the gin, lemon juice, and sugar syrup
   vigorously over cracked ice until well frosted.
2. Strain into a chilled Collins glass and top off
   with club soda.
3. Dress with the lemon slice.

DEAUVILLE PASSION

SERVES 1

1¾ measures cognac
1¼ measures apricot curaçao
1¼ measures passion fruit juice
cracked ice cubes
bitter lemon
fresh mint leaves, to decorate

1. Shake the cognac, apricot curaçao, and passion
   fruit juice over cracked ice until well frosted.
2. Strain into a chilled glass, top off with bitter
   lemon, and dress with the mint leaves.

BVD

1 measure brandy
1 measure dry vermouth
1 measure Dubonnet
cracked ice cubes

1. Pour the brandy, vermouth, and Dubonnet over cracked ice in a mixing glass.
2. Stir to mix and strain into a chilled cocktail glass.

SIDECAR

2 measures brandy
1 measure Triple Sec
1 measure lemon juice
cracked ice cubes
orange zest strip, to decorate

1. Shake the brandy, Triple Sec, and lemon juice vigorously over cracked ice until well frosted.
2. Strain into a chilled lowball glass and dress with the orange zest.

RETRO

COSMOPOLITAN

SERVES I

THIS FASHIONABLE COCKTAIL, MADE FAMOUS BY THE TV SHOW *SEX AND THE CITY*, IS THE ONLY DRINK TO SERVE AT A TRENDY PARTY! IT IS A DELICIOUS COMBINATION OF CITRUS AND BERRY FLAVORS.

2 measures vodka
1 measure Triple Sec
1 measure lime juice
1 measure cranberry juice
cracked ice cubes
orange zest strip, to decorate

1. Shake all the liquid ingredients over cracked ice until well frosted.
2. Strain into a chilled cocktail glass.
3. Dress with the orange zest.

Woo-Woo

SERVES 1

BE SURE TO WOO YOUR FRIENDS WITH THIS REFRESHING AND SIMPLE
DRINK. ITS FRUITY FLAVOR MAKES IT INCREDIBLY EASY TO DRINK,
YET IT STILL PACKS A PUNCH IN THE ALCOHOL STAKES!

cracked ice cubes
2 measures vodka
2 measures peach schnapps
4 measures cranberry juice
cape gooseberry, to decorate

1. Fill a chilled cocktail glass halfway with cracked ice.
2. Pour the vodka, peach schnapps, and cranberry juice over the ice.
3. Stir well to mix and dress with the cape gooseberry.

SCREWDRIVER

SERVES 1

cracked ice cubes
2 measures vodka
orange juice
orange slice, to decorate

1. Fill a chilled glass with cracked ice.
2. Pour the vodka over the ice and top off with orange juice.
3. Stir well to mix and dress with the orange slice.

GIN CUP

SERVES 1

cracked ice cubes
2 measures Pimm's No. 1
lemon-flavored soda pop
fresh mint sprigs and orange, lemon, and
    cucumber slices, to decorate

1. Fill a tall glass two-thirds full with cracked ice and pour in the Pimm's No. 1.
2. Top off with soda pop and stir gently.
3. Dress with the mint sprigs and orange, lemon, and cucumber slices.

HARVEY WALLBANGER

cracked ice cubes
3 measures vodka
8 measures orange juice
2 tsp Galliano
cocktail cherry and orange slice,
   to decorate

1. Fill a tall glass halfway with cracked ice, pour
    in the vodka and orange juice, and float the
    Galliano on top.
2. Dress with the cocktail cherry and orange
    slice.

CHERRY COLA

SERVES 1

cracked ice cubes
2 measures cherry brandy
1 measure lemon juice
cola

1. Fill a chilled lowball glass with
    cracked ice. Pour the brandy and
    lemon juice over the ice.
2. Top off with cola and stir gently.

SEX ON THE BEACH

SERVES 1

VACATION DRINKS ARE OFTEN FRESH AND FRUITY AND
THIS REFRESHING COCKTAIL IS REMINISCENT OF LONG, HOT SUMMER
DAYS — AND NIGHTS!

1 measure peach schnapps
1 measure vodka
2 measures orange juice
3 measures cranberry and
   peach juice
cracked and crushed ice cubes
dash lemon juice
thinly pared orange rind,
   to decorate

1. Shake the peach schnapps, vodka, orange juice, and cranberry and peach juice over cracked ice until well frosted.
2. Strain into a glass filled with crushed ice and squeeze over the lemon juice.
3. Dress with the orange rind.

FUZZY NAVEL

SERVES I

THE NAME OF THIS COCKTAIL PLAYS ON THE INGREDIENTS—FUZZY
TO REMIND YOU THAT IT CONTAINS PEACH SCHNAPPS AND NAVEL
BECAUSE IT IS MIXED WITH ORANGE JUICE.

2 measures vodka
1 measure peach schnapps
8 measures orange juice
cracked ice cubes
cape gooseberry, to decorate

1. Shake the vodka, peach schnapps, and orange juice vigorously over cracked ice until well frosted.
2. Strain into a chilled cocktail glass and dress with the cape gooseberry.

Origins of the Word "Cocktail"

THERE ARE AS MANY THEORIES ABOUT THE ORIGINS OF THE WORD "COCKTAIL" AS THERE ARE COCKTAILS THEMSELVES AND EVERY BARMAN WORTH HIS SHAKER KNOWS ENOUGH OF THEM TO KEEP YOU ENTERTAINED THROUGH AT LEAST THREE GOOD MARTINIS!

Here are a few of our favorites:

 It used to be fashionable to put a feather in one's drink as both decoration and a sign to teetotalers that the drink contained alcohol. As cock's tail feathers were both colorful and easy to come by, theirs were the preferred garnish.

 In 1936, the *Bartender* magazine published a story of English sailors in Mexico being served drinks stirred with a *Cola de Gallo*—a long root similar in shape to a cock's tail.

 Also in Mexico, the word is said to be a derivation from the Mexican princess Xochitl, who served drinks to American soldiers. As there was not enough of each spirit to accommodate all of their tastes, she simply mixed them all together.

 Another theory is that the word is derived from *coquetier*, a kind of French egg cup popular in bars in New Orleans in the early 1800s.

According to another tall tale, cocktails are named in honor of an American tavern keeper who stored his home-mixed drinks in a special ceramic container shaped like a rooster. Thirsty patrons would tap the cock's tail for service.

It is said that 18th-century fighting cocks would be given a mixture of gin and brandy to make them aggressive before a fight. The blend was known as "cocks' ale."

During the War of Independence, revolutionary American and French troops in New York State would drink together. The Americans preferred whiskey and gin and the French favored wine and vermouth. One night, one of them stole a rooster from the tavern owner's neighbor, a suspected supporter of the British enemy. The bird was cooked and served to the soldiers, who celebrated by mixing their drinks together and adorning them with the tail feathers. The toasts were "Vive le cock tail!"

The 1965 book *The Booze Reader: A Soggy Saga of Man in His Cups* by George Bishop has the less romantic definition: "The word itself stems from the English cock-tail which, in the mid-1800s, referred to a woman of easy virtue who was desirable but impure…and applied to the newly acquired American habit of bastardizing good British gin with foreign matter, including ice."

Banana Daiquiri

~ Serves 1 ~

2 measures white rum
½ measure Triple Sec
½ measure lime juice
½ measure light cream
1 tsp sugar syrup
¼ banana, peeled and sliced
lime wedge, to decorate

1. In a blender, process the rum, Triple Sec, lime juice, cream, sugar syrup, and banana until smooth.
2. Pour the mixture, without straining, into a chilled lowball glass and dress with the lime wedge.

Peach Daiquiri

~ Serves 1 ~

2 measures white rum
1 measure lime juice
½ tsp sugar syrup
½ peach, peeled, pitted, and chopped

1. In a blender, process the rum, lime juice, sugar syrup, and peach until smooth.
2. Pour the mixture, without straining, into a chilled lowball glass.

STRAWBERRY COLADA

crushed ice cubes
3 measures golden rum
4 measures pineapple juice
1 measure coconut cream
6 strawberries, hulled
pineapple wedge and whole strawberry,
    to decorate

1. In a blender, process the crushed ice, rum,
   pineapple juice, coconut cream, and hulled
   strawberries until smooth.
2. Pour the mixture, without straining, into a
   chilled highball glass.
3. Dress with the pineapple wedge and whole
   strawberry.

BANANA COLADA

crushed ice cubes
2 measures white rum
4 measures pineapple juice
1 measure Malibu
1 banana, peeled and sliced
pineapple wedges, to decorate

1. In a blender, process the crushed
   ice, rum, pineapple juice, Malibu,
   and banana until smooth.
2. Pour the mixture, without straining, into a
   chilled highball glass.
3. Dress with the pineapple wedges.

SANGRIA

SERVES 6

THIS SPANISH CLASSIC, A REFRESHING CONCOCTION OF RED WINE,
SODA POP, AND CITRUS FRUITS, IS IDEAL FOR A SIZZLING
SUMMER'S DAY. IT IS THE PERFECT CROWD-PLEASER AT ANY FIESTA.

juice 1 orange
juice 1 lemon
2 tbsp confectioners' sugar
cracked ice cubes
1 orange, thinly sliced
1 lemon, thinly sliced
1 bottle red wine, chilled
lemon-flavored soda pop

1. Shake the orange and lemon juice with the sugar and transfer to a large bowl or pitcher.
2. When the sugar has dissolved, add a few cracked ice cubes, the sliced fruit, and the wine.
3. Let stand for 1 hour if possible, and then add soda pop to taste and more ice.

SEABREEZE

SERVES 1

PINK GRAPEFRUIT JUICE IS MUCH SWEETER AND SUBTLER THAN ITS
PALER COUSIN, SO IT IS IDEAL TO MIX IN COCKTAILS WHERE YOU
WANT JUST A SLIGHT SHARPNESS.

1½ measures vodka
½ measure cranberry juice
cracked ice cubes
pink grapefruit juice

1. Shake the vodka and cranberry juice over cracked ice until frosted.
2. Pour into a chilled highball glass and top off with grapefruit juice.

CLUB MOJITO

SERVES I

1 tsp sugar syrup
a few fresh mint leaves, plus extra to decorate
juice ½ lime
cracked ice cubes
2 measures Jamaican rum
club soda
dash Angostura bitters

1. Put the sugar syrup, mint leaves, and lime juice in a lowball glass and mash the mint leaves with a muddler or spoon.
2. Add cracked ice cubes and the rum, then top off with club soda.
3. Finish with the Angostura bitters and dress with the mint leaves.

MISSISSIPPI MULE

SERVES I

2 measures gin
½ measure crème de cassis
½ measure lemon juice
cracked ice cubes

1. Shake the gin, crème de cassis, and lemon juice vigorously over cracked ice until well frosted.
2. Strain into a chilled lowball glass.

SES

2 measures sloe gin
orange juice
cracked ice cubes
orange slice, to decorate

1. Shake the gin and orange juice over cracked ice until well frosted and pour into a chilled glass.
2. Decorate with the orange slice.

BLUE LAGOON

1 measure blue curaçao
1 measure vodka
dash lemon juice
lemon-flavored soda pop

1. Pour the curaçao into a chilled highball or cocktail glass, followed by the vodka.
2. Add the lemon juice and top off with soda pop.

SHADY LADY

THIS IS ONE OF THE BEST TEQUILA COCKTAILS OF ALL TIME. DARK AND MYSTERIOUS, IT IS DEFINITELY A DRINK TO BE ENJOYED IN THE TWILIGHT HOURS.

3 measures tequila
1 measure applejack
1 measure cranberry juice
dash lime juice
cracked ice cubes

1. Shake the tequila, applejack, cranberry juice, and lime juice over cracked ice until well frosted.
2. Strain into a chilled cocktail glass.

Orange Blossom

Serves 1

During the Prohibition years, gin was often quite literally made in the bathtub and had to be mixed with orange juice to conceal its filthy flavor. Made with good-quality gin, this drink is delightfully refreshing.

2 measures gin
2 measures orange juice
cracked ice cubes
orange slice, to decorate

1. Shake the gin and orange juice vigorously over cracked ice until well frosted.
2. Strain into a chilled cocktail glass and dress with the orange slice.

CRANBERRY COLLINS

SERVES 1

2 measures vodka
¾ measure elderflower cordial
3 measures white cranberry and apple juice
cracked ice cubes
club soda
cranberries and lime slices, to decorate

1. Shake the vodka, elderflower cordial, and cranberry and apple juice over cracked ice until well frosted.
2. Strain into a Collins glass with more ice and top off with club soda.
3. Dress with the cranberries and lime slice.

MELON BALL

SERVES 1

2 measures vodka
2 measures Midori
4 measures pineapple juice
cracked ice cubes
melon wedge, to decorate

1. Pour the vodka, Midori, and pineapple juice over cracked ice and stir well to mix.
2. Fill a chilled highball glass halfway with cracked ice and strain over the cocktail.
3. Dress with the melon wedge.

Island Blues

lemon wedge
granulated sugar
¾ measure peach schnapps
½ measure blue curaçao
1 small egg white
dash lemon juice
cracked ice cubes
lemon-flavored soda pop

1. Rub the rim of a chilled glass with the lemon wedge, then dip in a saucer of sugar to frost.
2. Place the peach schnapps, blue curaçao, egg white, and lemon juice into a cocktail shaker with cracked ice.
3. Shake well and strain into the glass.
4. Top off with soda pop.

Jocose Julep

4–6 ice cubes, crushed
3 measures bourbon whiskey
1 measure green crème de menthe
1½ measures lime juice
1 tsp sugar syrup
5 fresh mint leaves, plus an extra sprig to decorate
cracked ice cubes
sparkling water

1. In a blender, process the crushed ice, bourbon, crème de menthe, lime juice, sugar syrup, and mint leaves until smooth.
2. Fill a chilled lowball glass with cracked ice and pour in the cocktail. Top off with sparkling water and stir gently.
3. Dress with the mint sprig.

Pink Squirrel

Serves 1

CRÈME DE NOYAUX HAS A WONDERFUL, SLIGHTLY BITTER, NUTTY
FLAVOR, BUT IS, IN FACT, MADE FROM PEACH AND APRICOT KERNELS.
IT IS USUALLY SERVED AS A LIQUEUR, BUT DOES COMBINE WELL
WITH SOME OTHER INGREDIENTS IN COCKTAILS.

2 measures dark crème de cacao
1 measure crème de noyaux
1 measure light cream
cracked ice cubes

1. Shake the crème de cacao, crème
    de noyaux, and light cream
    vigorously over cracked ice until
    well frosted.
2. Strain into a chilled glass.

FLYING GRASSHOPPER

SERVES 1

THERE ARE TWO VERSIONS OF THIS COCKTAIL—ONE MADE
WITH EQUAL QUANTITIES OF WHITE AND GREEN CRÈME DE
MENTHE AND THIS ONE WITH GREEN CRÈME DE MENTHE AND
CHOCOLATE LIQUEUR.

cracked ice cubes
1 measure vodka
1 measure green crème
   de menthe
1 measure crème de cacao

1. Put the cracked ice into a mixing
   glass or pitcher and pour in the
   vodka, crème de menthe, and
   crème de cacao.
2. Stir well and strain into a
   chilled cocktail glass.

CAIPIRINHA

SERVES I

THIS CLASSIC BRAZILIAN COCKTAIL IS BASED ON THE SUGARCANE
SPIRIT CACHAÇA, MUDDLED WITH LIME AND SUGAR. IF YOU FIND IT
TOO SHARP, ADD A LITTLE MORE SUGAR.

6 lime wedges, plus extra
  to decorate
2 tsp granulated sugar
3 measures cachaça
cracked ice cubes

1. Put the lime wedges and sugar in
   a chilled lowball glass and mash
   with a muddler or spoon to release
   the lime juice.
2. Pour on the cachaça, fill up the
   glass with cracked ice, and stir
   well. Dress with the lime wedge.

PEARTINI

SERVES 1

WHILE LESS POPULAR THAN PEACH OR CHERRY EAU DE VIE, PEAR
BRANDY HAS A DELICATE FRAGRANCE AND LOVELY FLAVOR, BUT
DON'T CONFUSE IT WITH PEAR LIQUEUR.

1 tsp granulated sugar
pinch ground cinnamon
lemon wedge
cracked ice cubes
1 measure vodka
1 measure pear brandy

1. Mix the sugar and cinnamon in a saucer. Rub the rim of a chilled cocktail glass with the lemon wedge, then dip it into the sugar-and-cinnamon mixture.
2. Put the cracked ice into a mixing glass and pour in the vodka and pear brandy. Stir well and strain into the glass.

Vodkatini

1 measure vodka
cracked ice cubes
dash dry vermouth
lemon zest strip, to decorate

1. Pour the vodka over cracked ice in a mixing glass.
2. Add the vermouth, stir well, and strain into a chilled cocktail glass.
3. Dress with the lemon zest.

Vodka Espresso

cracked ice cubes
2 measures espresso or other strong black coffee, cooled
1 measure vodka
2 tsp superfine sugar
1 measure Amarula

1. Put the cracked ice into a cocktail shaker, pour in the coffee and vodka, and add the sugar.
2. Shake vigorously until well frosted.
3. Strain into a chilled cocktail glass, then float the Amarula on top.

CHOCOLATE MARTINI

lemon wedge
unsweetened cocoa
2 measures vodka
¼ measure crème de cacao
2 dashes orange flower water
cracked ice cubes

1. Rub the rim of a chilled cocktail glass with the lemon wedge, then dip in a saucer of cocoa.
2. Shake the vodka, crème de cacao, and orange flower water over cracked ice until well frosted.
3. Strain into the glass.

APPLE MARTINI

cracked ice cubes
1 measure vodka
1 measure sour apple schnapps
1 measure apple juice

1. Put the cracked ice into a cocktail shaker and pour in the vodka, schnapps, and apple juice.
2. Shake vigorously until well frosted.
3. Strain into a chilled cocktail glass.

Metropolitan

Serves I

This sophisticated cocktail for city slickers shares its name, but not its ingredients, with an equally urbane classic from the past.

lemon wedge
granulated sugar
cracked ice cubes
½ measure vodka or lemon vodka
½ measure framboise liqueur
½ measure cranberry juice
½ measure orange juice
cranberries, to decorate

1. Rub the rim of a chilled cocktail glass with the lemon wedge, then dip in a saucer of sugar to frost.
2. Put the cracked ice into a cocktail shaker and pour in the vodka, framboise, cranberry juice, and orange juice. Cover and shake vigorously until well frosted.
3. Strain into the glass and dress with the cranberries.

WHITE COSMOPOLITAN

SERVES 1

THIS COCKTAIL IS NOTHING LIKE ITS PINK COUSIN THE
COSMOPOLITAN, BECAUSE IT IS FAR MORE FRUITY AND INSTEAD OF
VODKA, IT IS BASED ON A PUNCHY LEMON-FLAVORED LIQUEUR.

1½ measures Limoncello
½ measure Cointreau
1 measure white cranberry and
  grape juice
cracked ice cubes
dash orange bitters
cranberries, to decorate

1. Shake the Limoncello, Cointreau,
   and cranberry and grape juice over
   cracked ice until well frosted.
2. Strain into a chilled glass.
3. Add the bitters and dress with the
   cranberries.

Famous Cocktail Bars of the World

COCKTAILS WERE ALWAYS MEANT TO BE ENJOYED IN COMPANY AND MANY OF THE MOST CELEBRATED CONCOCTIONS WE DRINK NOW WERE CREATED IN HISTORIC BARS FREQUENTED BY THE RICH AND FAMOUS WHERE YOU CAN STILL TASTE THE GLAMOUR TODAY.

The Savoy, London

The famous five-star hotel is also home to one of the most revered cocktail bars in the world. In 1898, the American Bar at the Savoy opened and introduced Europe to the delights of the cocktail. The first head bartender, Ada Coleman, created drinks for the likes of Mark Twain and the Prince of Wales. Her successor, Harry Craddock, became the most celebrated mixologist of the 1920s and 1930s, inventing a number of cocktails, including the White Lady, and helping to popularize the Dry Martini. In 1930, he published the definitive *Savoy Cocktail Book*, which is still available today.

King Cole Bar, New York

This bar, at the upscale St. Regis Hotel in midtown Manhattan, is credited as being the first American establishment to serve the Bloody Mary (then called the Red Snapper) after its invention in Harry's American Bar, Paris. Still a place to see and be seen, it maintains a reputation for some of the best cocktails in New York City.

Raffles Hotel Bar, Singapore

The luxurious colonial hotel opened in 1887 and the Long Bar is home to the Singapore Sling. Invented by barman Ngiam Tong Boon around 1910, the Raffles version of the cocktail is still recognized as the finest in the world, thanks to their use of their own club soda, and has been enjoyed by the likes of Noel Coward, Rudyard Kipling, Joseph Conrad, and Charlie Chaplin.

HARRY'S BAR, VENICE

First opened in 1931 by bartender Giuseppe Cipriani with money loaned to
him by American cocktail enthusiast Harry Pickering, this Venetian institution
lays claim to being the birthplace of the Bellini. It was invented by Giuseppe
and so named because its color reminded him of a saint's toga in a painting by
15th-century Venetian artist Giovanni Bellini. Charlie Chaplin, Orson Welles,
and Truman Capote were all regulars, and Ernest Hemingway is said to have
been the first person to order a Montgomery Martini (15 parts gin to one part
dry vermouth) here.

LA BODEGUITA DEL MEDIO, HAVANA

Known as the birthplace of the Mojito, supposedly invented here in 1942,
this jumbled, unpretentious bar in Havana now overflows with souvenirs and
mementoes of its famous clientele. For decades it has been the favored hangout
of poets, writers, actors, musicians, and journalists—most famous of them all is
Ernest Hemingway (again!), whose handwritten endorsement "Mi Mojito en la
Bodeguita" can still be seen on the wall.

HARRY'S AMERICAN BAR, PARIS

The bar at 5 Rue Danou was made famous by Harry MacElhone, who in
1923 turned the failing expat hangout into a world-renowned watering hole.
Yet another favorite of Ernest Hemingway's, its clientele also included Coco
Chanel, Humphrey Bogart, Rita Hayworth, and even the Duke of Windsor, all
of whom came for the signature cocktails. The Bloody Mary was invented here,
by barman Fernand Petiot, as well as the Sidecar XO, named after the mode of
transport employed by a regular Army General visitor.

Indian Summer

1 measure vodka
2 measures Kahlúa
1 measure gin
2 measures pineapple juice
cracked ice cubes
tonic water

1. Shake the vodka, Kahlúa, gin, and pineapple juice vigorously over cracked ice until frosted.
2. Strain into a chilled cocktail glass or wine glass and top off with tonic water.

Palm Beach

1 measure white rum
1 measure gin
1 measure pineapple juice
cracked ice cubes

1. Shake the rum, gin, and pineapple juice vigorously over ice until well frosted.
2. Strain into a chilled glass.

GODMOTHER

cracked ice cubes
2 measures vodka
1 measure Amaretto

1. Fill a chilled lowball glass halfway with cracked ice.
2. Pour the vodka and Amaretto over the ice.
3. Stir to mix.

BLACK BEAUTY

2 measures vodka
1 measure black sambuca
cracked ice cubes
black olive, to decorate

1. Stir the vodka and sambuca with cracked ice in a mixing glass until frosted.
2. Strain into a chilled cocktail glass and dress with the olive.

Purple Passion

Serves 1

This fruity cooler still has quite a kick at its heart.
Try using one of the citrus-flavored vodkas for a subtle
change in taste.

cracked ice cubes
2 measures vodka
4 measures grapefruit juice
4 measures purple grape juice

1. Fill a chilled highball glass with cracked ice.
2. Shake the vodka, grapefruit juice, and grape juice vigorously over cracked ice until well frosted.
3. Strain into the glass.

Costa Del Sol

Serves 1

The warm and fruity flavors in this fantastic cocktail are evocative of long summer days spent soaking up the Spanish sun.

cracked ice cubes
2 measures gin
1 measure apricot brandy
1 measure Triple Sec

1. Fill a chilled lowball glass halfway with cracked ice.
2. Shake the gin, apricot brandy, and Triple Sec vigorously over cracked ice until well frosted.
3. Strain into the glass.

COLLEEN

2 measures Irish whiskey
1 measure Irish Mist
1 measure Triple Sec
1 tsp lemon juice
cracked ice cubes

1. Shake the Irish whiskey, Irish Mist, Triple Sec, and lemon juice vigorously over cracked ice until well frosted.
2. Strain into a chilled cocktail glass.

RUM COCKTAIL

1 measure white rum
1 measure dark rum
1 measure Kahlúa
1 tsp lemon juice
2 tsp orange juice
cracked ice cubes
lime slice, to decorate

1. Shake the white rum, dark rum, Kahlúa, lemon juice, and orange juice vigorously over cracked ice until well frosted.
2. Strain into a chilled lowball glass. Dress with the lime slice.

Blue Monday

cracked ice cubes
1 measure vodka
½ measure Cointreau
1 tbsp blue curaçao

1. Put the cracked ice into a mixing glass and pour in the vodka, Cointreau, and curaçao.
2. Stir well and strain into a chilled cocktail glass.

Nirvana

2 measures dark rum
½ measure grenadine
½ measure tamarind syrup
1 tsp sugar syrup
cracked ice cubes
grapefruit juice

1. Shake the rum, grenadine, tamarind syrup, and sugar syrup vigorously over cracked ice until well frosted.
2. Fill a chilled glass halfway with cracked ice and strain over the cocktail.
3. Top off with grapefruit juice.

BLACK WIDOW

SERVES 1

THIS DRINK IS NOT QUITE AS WICKED AS ITS NAME SUGGESTS, BUT IF
YOU ARE FEELING ADVENTUROUS YOU COULD TAKE IT STRAIGHT, ON
THE ROCKS!

⅔ measure dark rum
⅓ measure Southern Comfort
juice ½ lime
dash curaçao
cracked ice cubes
club soda
thinly pared lime rind,
　to decorate

1. Shake the rum, Southern
   Comfort, lime juice, and curaçao
   vigorously over cracked ice until
   frosted.
2. Strain into a chilled lowball glass
   and top off with club soda.
3. Dress with the lime rind.

GRAND BAHAMA

SERVES I

THE CARIBBEAN IS HOME TO SOME OF THE WORLD'S FINEST RUMS,
SO IT IS ONLY NATURAL THAT ONE OF ITS ISLANDS SHOULD GIVE ITS
NAME TO THIS FABULOUS RUM COCKTAIL.

1 measure white rum
½ measure brandy
1 measure Triple Sec
1 measure lime juice
cracked ice cubes
lime slice, to decorate

1. Shake the rum, brandy, Triple Sec, and lime juice vigorously over cracked ice until well frosted.
2. Strain into a chilled cocktail glass.
3. Dress with the lime slice.

Adam & Eve

Serves 1

2 measures Triple Sec
1 measure vodka
1 measure grapefruit juice
1 measure cranberry juice
cracked ice cubes
5–6 pineapple cubes
2 tsp confectioners' sugar
1–2 tbsp crushed ice cubes
strawberry, to decorate

1. Shake the Triple Sec, vodka, grapefruit juice, and cranberry juice over cracked ice until well frosted.
2. Strain into a chilled glass.
3. In a blender, process the pineapple with the sugar and crushed ice until smooth.
4. Float gently on the top of the cocktail.
5. Dress with the strawberry.

Paradise

Serves 1

cracked ice cubes
1 measure gin
½ measure apricot brandy
½ measure orange juice
dash lemon juice

1. Put the cracked ice in a cocktail shaker and pour in the gin, apricot brandy, orange juice, and lemon juice.
2. Shake vigorously until well frosted.
3. Strain into a chilled lowball glass.

XYZ

SERVES 1

½ measure lemon juice
½ measure white rum
½ measure Cointreau
cracked ice cubes
lime slice, to decorate

1. Shake all the liquid ingredients together over cracked ice until well frosted.
2. Strain into a chilled glass and dress with the lime slice.

GREYHOUND

SERVES 1

cracked ice cubes
1½ measures vodka or lemon vodka
6 measures grapefruit juice

1. Put the cracked ice in a highball glass and pour in the vodka and grapefruit juice.
2. Stir well.

Ginger Beer

Serves 1

Yes, it's ginger beer, but it's nothing like the alcohol-free ginger ale you may have drunk as a child. The ginger brandy adds a subtle warmth that is not too fiery.

1 cup beer
2 measures ginger brandy

1. Pour the beer into a chilled beer glass or tankard, then add the ginger brandy.

ZANDER

A LICORICE-FLAVORED LIQUEUR, SAMBUCA IS TRADITIONALLY DRUNK
STRAIGHT, BUT ITS INTENSE FLAVOR IS GREAT WITH FRUIT DRINKS,
AND MAKES A CHANGE FOR A LONG DRINK.

cracked ice cubes
1 measure sambuca
1 measure orange juice
dash lemon juice
bitter lemon

1. Fill a highball glass with cracked
   ice.
2. Shake the sambuca, orange juice,
   and lemon juice vigorously over
   cracked ice. Strain into the glass.
3. Top off with bitter lemon.

Pina Colada

SERVES 1

ONE OF THE YOUNGER GENERATION OF CLASSICS, THIS BECAME
POPULAR DURING THE COCKTAIL REVIVAL OF THE 1980S AND HAS
REMAINED SO EVER SINCE.

crushed ice cubes
2 measures white rum
1 measure dark rum
3 measures pineapple juice
2 measures coconut cream
pineapple wedges, to decorate

1. Process the crushed ice in a blender with the white rum, dark rum, pineapple juice, and coconut cream until smooth.
2. Pour, without straining, into a chilled tall glass and dress with the pineapple wedges.

MAI TAI

SERVES 1

CREATED IN 1944 BY RESTAURATEUR "TRADER VIC" THIS COCKTAIL
WAS DESCRIBED AS "MAI TAI—ROE AE" ROUGHLY TRANSLATING AS
"OUT OF THIS WORLD." IT IS ALWAYS FLAMBOYANTLY DRESSED.

2 measures white rum
2 measures dark rum
1 measure orange curaçao
1 measure lime juice
1 tbsp orgeat syrup
1 tbsp grenadine
cracked ice cubes
pineapple wedges, cocktail
   cherries, and thinly pared
   orange rind, to decorate

1. Shake the white rum, dark rum, curaçao, lime juice, orgeat syrup, and grenadine vigorously over cracked ice until well frosted.
2. Strain into a chilled cocktail glass and dress with pineapple wedges, cocktail cherries, and orange rind.

Singapore Sling

cracked ice cubes
2 measures gin
1 measure cherry brandy
1 measure lemon juice
1 tsp grenadine
club soda
lime zest strips and cocktail cherries,
    to decorate

1. Fill a chilled glass halfway with cracked ice.
2. Shake the gin, cherry brandy, lemon juice,
    and grenadine vigorously over cracked ice
    until well frosted.
3. Strain the cocktail into the glass.
4. Top off with club soda and dress with the lime
    zest and cocktail cherries.

Pineapple Punch

1 measure white rum
1 measure pineapple juice
juice ½ lime
½ measure curaçao
dash maraschino liqueur
cracked ice cubes
kiwi and pineapple wedges, to decorate

1. Put the rum, pineapple juice, lime juice,
    curaçao, maraschino liqueur, and cracked ice
    into a highball glass. Stir well.
2. Dress with the kiwi and pineapple wedges.

Japanese Slipper

cracked ice cubes
1½ measures vodka
1½ measures Midori
1 measure lime juice
lime slice, to decorate

1. Put the cracked ice into a cocktail shaker and pour in the vodka, Midori, and lime juice.
2. Shake vigorously until well frosted.
3. Strain into a chilled wine glass and dress with the lime slice.

Mimi

2 measures vodka
½ measure coconut cream
2 measures pineapple juice
crushed ice cubes
pineapple wedge, to decorate

1. Process the vodka, coconut cream, pineapple juice, and crushed ice in a blender for a few seconds until frothy.
2. Pour into a chilled cocktail glass and dress with the pineapple wedge.

Fuzzy Martini

Serves 1

VODKA COMBINES SO WONDERFULLY WITH OTHER LIQUORS THAT IT IS
NO WONDER THAT THE CLASSIC VODKA MARTINI HAS UNDERGONE SO
MANY INCARNATIONS. THIS VERSION INCLUDES PEACH SCHNAPPS.

2 measures vanilla vodka
½ measure coffee vodka
1 tsp peach schnapps
cracked ice cubes
peach slice, to decorate

1. Shake the vanilla vodka, coffee vodka, and peach schnapps over cracked ice until well frosted.
2. Strain into a chilled cocktail glass and dress with the peach slice.

LAST MANGO IN PARIS

SERVES 1

THE NAME OF THIS COCKTAIL ALLUDES TO THE 1972 FILM, STARRING
MARLON BRANDO AND MARIA SCHNEIDER. THINGS MIGHT HAVE
TURNED OUT DIFFERENTLY IF BRANDO HAD GONE FOR THE MANGO
INSTEAD OF THE TANGO.

2 measures vodka
1 measure framboise liqueur
1 measure lime juice
½ mango, peeled, pitted, and
  chopped
2 strawberries, hulled
lime slice, to decorate

1. In a blender, process all the
    ingredients until slushy.
2. Pour into a chilled glass
    and dress with the lime slice.

Fat Man Running

2 measures dark rum
½ measure blue curaçao
½ measure lime juice
cracked ice cubes
ginger ale

1. In a blender, process the rum, curaçao, lime juice, and cracked ice until slushy.
2. Pour into a highball glass and top off with ginger ale.

Cherry Kitch

1 measure cherry brandy
2 measures pineapple juice
½ measure Kirsch
1 egg white
crushed ice cubes
cocktail cherry, to decorate

1. Shake the cherry brandy, pineapple juice, Kirsch, and egg white vigorously over crushed ice until frosted.
2. Strain into a chilled tall glass and dress with the cocktail cherry.

OCEAN BREEZE

SERVES 1

1 measure white rum
1 measure amaretto
½ measure blue curaçao
½ measure pineapple juice
crushed ice cubes
club soda

1. Shake the rum, amaretto, curaçao, and
   pineapple juice vigorously over crushed ice.
2. Strain into a chilled tall glass and top off with
   club soda.

MOONLIGHT

SERVES 2

3 measures grapefruit juice
4 measures gin
1 measure Kirsch
4 measures white wine
½ tsp grated lemon rind
cracked ice cubes

1. Shake all the ingredients well
   over cracked ice and strain into
   chilled glasses.

Cocktails in the Movies

COCKTAILS ARE INEXTRICABLY LINKED TO HOLLYWOOD, NOT ONLY SHARING THE SAME GLAMOUR AND MYSTIQUE BUT ALSO FEATURING IN SOME OF THE MOST FAMOUS FILMS OF ALL TIME.

JAMES BOND

007 may be most famous for his "Dry Martini, shaken not stirred," but in his 2006 film, *Casino Royale*, the world's most famous spy added a twist to the tale. During the multimillion dollar poker game at the climax of the film, Bond takes a break to order a drink, instructing the barman exactly how to mix it. "Three measures of Gordon's, one of vodka, half a measure of Kina Lillet. Shake over ice, and then add a thin slice of lemon peel." He dubs this Martini variant the Vesper, after his female companion, and when the barman asks if he would like it shaken or stirred, delivers the best line of the film: "Do I look like I give a damn?"

CASABLANCA

There's a lot of drinking in Rick's Café and the most famous bar in all film history also serves up a mean champagne cocktail. Who could forget Humphrey Bogart's toast, "Here's looking at you, kid," as he mixes Ingrid Bergman a concoction made of dry champagne, brandy, a sugar cube, and Angostura bitters?

SEX AND THE CITY

The quartet of New York girl pals introduced a whole generation of women to the delights of the Cosmopolitan—a cocktail created as recently as 1985—especially narrator Carrie Bradshaw, for whom it was the only drink to be seen with. "Hi, I'd like a cheeseburger please, large fries, and a Cosmopolitan," she deadpans, at a stroke making it the essential drink for any girls' night out.

THE BIG LEBOWSKI

The cult film starring Jeff Bridges as "The Dude" sparked a massive increase in popularity for White Russians, as his character knocks back no less than nine of the drinks throughout the movie. Perhaps the most memorable of those is as he attempts to keep sipping from his glass while being strong-armed by a thug: "Careful man," he drawls, "there's a beverage here…"

THE NUTTY PROFESSOR

We're talking about the 1963 original, of course, and not the 1996 Eddie Murphy remake. In this classic comedy, Jerry Lewis ad-libs a cocktail of his own design to the bartender: "Two shots of vodka, a little rum, some bitters, and a smidgen of vinegar… a shot of vermouth, a shot of gin, a little brandy, lemon peel, orange peel, cherry, some more Scotch. Now mix it nice and pour it into a tall glass." He calls it the Alaskan Polar Bear Heater. The barman asks if he intends to drink it here, "or are you going to take it home and rub it onto your chest?"

COCKTAIL

Tom Cruise as the mixmaster with the magic hands and a winning way with a shaker introduced a whole generation of new drinkers to the delights of an extravagantly presented tipple. Unfortunately, although the 1988 film was a smash at the box office—and to be fair to Cruise, did include some impressive mixing routines—it wasn't exactly Oscar-winning stuff and perhaps is best summed up in its star's rather embarrassingly sung ode to the delights of a London gin: "Gordon's is my favorite drink. It's very easy to sink, sink, sink. And we'll drink it now, we'll drink it then. We'll drink it till we cause mayhem. Mayhem, mayhem, mayhem."

Golden Frog

GALLIANO AND STREGA ARE ITALIAN HERBAL LIQUEURS THAT ARE
BOTH A VIVID YELLOW COLOR, HENCE THE NAME OF THIS COCKTAIL.
THIS IS ONE FROG YOU'LL BE WILLING TO GET YOUR LIPS AROUND!

4–6 cracked ice cubes
1 measure vodka
1 measure Strega
1 measure Galliano
1 measure lemon juice

1. Process the cracked ice in a
   blender with the vodka, Strega,
   Galliano, and lemon juice until
   slushy.
2. Pour into a chilled cocktail glass.

CROCODILE

SERVES 1

THIS IS CERTAINLY A SNAPPY COCKTAIL WITH A BIT OF BITE.
IT PROBABLY GETS THE NAME FROM ITS SPECTACULAR COLOR, A
STARTLING SHADE OF GREEN, PROVIDED BY THE JAPANESE MELON-
FLAVORED LIQUEUR, MIDORI.

2 measures vodka
1 measure Triple Sec
1 measure Midori
2 measures lemon juice
cracked ice cubes

1. Pour the vodka, Triple Sec, Midori, and lemon juice over cracked ice and shake vigorously until well frosted.
2. Strain into a chilled glass.

STRAWBERRINI

SERVES 1

6 fresh or frozen strawberries
1 tbsp confectioners' sugar
1–2 drops lime juice
splash fraise liqueur
2 measures vodka, well iced

1. Reserve 1–2 strawberries to add later.
2. Crush the remaining strawberries in a bowl with the sugar, lime juice, and fraise liqueur. Strain well.
3. Pour the vodka into a chilled martini glass and add the puree. Dress with the reserved strawberries.

RASPBERRINI

SERVES 1

10 fresh or frozen raspberries
1 tbsp confectioners' sugar
1–2 drops lemon juice
splash framboise liqueur
2 measures vodka, well iced

1. Reserve 4–5 raspberries to add later.
2. Crush the remaining raspberries in a bowl with the sugar, lemon, and framboise liqueur. Strain well.
3. Pour the vodka into a chilled cocktail glass and add the puree. Dress with the reserved raspberries.

SPOTTED BIKINI

1 ripe passion fruit
2 measures vodka
1 measure white rum
1 measure cold milk
juice ½ lemon
cracked ice cubes
thinly pared lemon rind, to decorate

1. Scoop out the passion fruit flesh into a pitcher.
2. Shake the vodka, rum, milk, and lemon juice over cracked ice until well frosted.
3. Strain into a chilled cocktail glass and add the passion fruit, not strained, at the last minute.
4. Dress with the lemon rind.

CREAMY SCREWDRIVER

cracked and crushed ice cubes
2 measures vodka
6 measures orange juice
1 egg yolk
½ tsp sugar syrup
orange slice, to decorate

1. Fill a chilled highball glass halfway with cracked ice.
2. In a blender, process the vodka, orange juice, egg yolk, sugar syrup, and crushed ice until smooth.
3. Pour, without straining, into the prepared glass.
4. Dress with the orange slice.

Lemon Sherbet

Serves 1

STRICTLY FOR ADULTS ONLY, THIS DRINK IS A DELICIOUSLY THICK
AND FLUFFY CONCOCTION THAT IS BEST DRUNK THROUGH STRAWS
OR, BETTER STILL, EATEN WITH A SPOON!

2 measures gin
1 measure lemon juice
1 measure light cream
½ measure orange curaçao
1 tsp superfine sugar
dash orange flower water
crushed ice cubes

1. In a blender, process all
    the ingredients together for
    10–15 seconds, until smooth.
2. Pour into a chilled highball glass.

SLOE GIN RICKEY

SERVES I

THE ORIGINAL GIN RICKEY IS MADE WITH REGULAR GIN, WHICH IS
FLAVORED WITH JUNIPER BERRY OIL. HERE THE SLOE GIN MAKES IT A
SLIGHTLY SWEETER, BUT STILL SHARP AND REFRESHING, DRINK.

cracked ice cubes
2 measures sloe gin
2 measures lime juice
club soda
lime slice, to decorate

1. Fill a highball glass halfway with cracked ice.
2. Pour in the sloe gin and lime juice and top off with club soda.
3. Dress with the lime slice.

The Blues

1½ measures tequila
½ measure maraschino liqueur
½ measure blue curaçao
½ measure lemon juice
cracked ice cubes
bitter lemon

1. Shake the tequila, maraschino liqueur, curaçao, and lemon juice vigorously over cracked ice until frosted.
2. Strain into a chilled lowball glass and top off with bitter lemon.

Bachelor's Bait

2 measures gin
1 tsp grenadine
1 egg white
cracked ice cubes
dash orange bitters

1. Shake the gin, grenadine, and egg white vigorously over cracked ice until well frosted.
2. Add the orange bitters, give the mixture another quick shake, and strain into a chilled cocktail glass.

Brandy Sour

1 measure lime or lemon juice
2½ measures brandy
1 tsp superfine sugar or sugar syrup
cracked ice cubes
lime slice and cocktail cherry, to decorate

1. Shake the lime juice, brandy, and sugar
   vigorously over cracked ice until well frosted.
2. Strain into a chilled cocktail glass.
3. Dress with the lime slice and cocktail cherry.

Hawaiian Orange Blossom

2 measures gin
1 measure Triple Sec
2 measures orange juice
1 measure pineapple juice
cracked ice cubes
pineapple wedge and leaf, to decorate

1. Shake the gin, Triple Sec,
   orange juice, and pineapple
   juice vigorously over cracked
   ice until well frosted.
2. Strain into a chilled wine glass.
3. Dress with the pineapple wedge and leaf.

CHELSEA SIDECAR

SERVES 1

SO STRONG ARE THIS COCKTAIL'S ASSOCIATIONS WITH THE FAMOUS
ARTISTS' AND WRITERS' HANGOUT IN NEW YORK THAT IT'S
SOMETIMES KNOWN AS A CHELSEA HOTEL.

2 measures gin
1 measure Triple Sec
1 measure lemon juice
cracked ice cubes
lemon zest strip, to decorate

1. Pour the gin, Triple Sec, and
    lemon juice over cracked ice
    and shake vigorously until
    well frosted.
2. Strain into a chilled cocktail glass
    and dress with the lemon zest.

BOSTON SIDECAR

SERVES 1

A BOSTON SIDECAR DIFFERS FROM THE CLASSIC SIDECAR COCKTAIL
IN THAT IT INCLUDES RUM AS WELL AS THE USUAL BRANDY BASE.
LIME JUICE MAY BE USED IN PLACE OF THE LEMON JUICE.

1½ measures white rum
½ measure brandy
½ measure Triple Sec
½ measure lemon juice
cracked ice cubes
orange zest strip, to decorate

1. Pour the white rum, brandy, Triple Sec, and lemon juice over cracked ice and shake vigorously until well frosted.
2. Strain into a chilled cocktail glass and dress with the orange zest.

DECADENT

BELLINI

SERVES I

THIS DELICIOUS CONCOCTION OF SWEET PEACH JUICE AND CHAMPAGNE
WAS CREATED AROUND 1943 BY GIUSEPPE CIPRIANI AT HARRY'S BAR
IN VENICE, WHERE IT REMAINS A BEST-SELLER TO THIS DAY.

lemon wedge
granulated sugar
1 measure peach juice
3 measures champagne, chilled

1. Rub the rim of a chilled
   champagne flute with the lemon
   wedge, then dip in a saucer of
   sugar to frost.
2. Pour the peach juice into the
   prepared glass.
3. Add the chilled champagne.

KIR ROYALE

SERVES 1

AS WITH THE BEST MUSTARD, CRÈME DE CASSIS PRODUCTION IS CENTERED ON THE FRENCH CITY OF DIJON. THIS COCKTAIL IS NAMED IN MEMORY OF A PARTISAN AND MAYOR OF THE CITY, FÉLIX KIR.

a few drops crème de cassis, or to taste
1 tbsp brandy (optional)
champagne, chilled

1. Pour the crème de cassis and brandy, if using, into a chilled champagne flute.
2. Wait a moment, and then gently pour in the champagne.

BUCK'S FIZZ

SERVES I

2 measures orange juice, chilled
2 measures champagne, chilled

1. Fill a chilled champagne flute halfway with the orange juice, then gently pour in the chilled champagne.

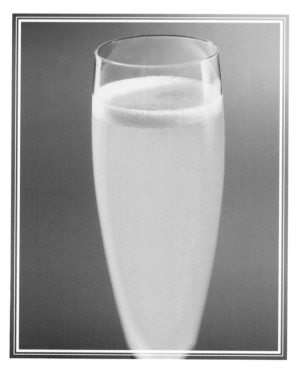

FLIRTINI

SERVES I

¼ slice fresh pineapple, chopped
½ measure Cointreau, chilled
½ measure vodka, chilled
1 measure pineapple juice, chilled
champagne or sparkling wine, chilled

1. Put the pineapple and Cointreau into a mixing glass and mash with a muddler or spoon to crush the pineapple.
2. Add the vodka and pineapple juice and stir well, then strain into a chilled glass. Top off with champagne.

MIMOSA

1 passion fruit
½ measure orange curaçao
crushed ice cubes
champagne, chilled
star fruit slice, to decorate

1. Scoop out the passion fruit flesh into a shaker
   and shake with the curaçao and crushed ice
   until frosted.
2. Pour into a chilled champagne flute and top
   off with champagne.
3. Dress with the star fruit slice.

CHAMPAGNE COCKTAIL

1 sugar cube
2 dashes Angostura bitters
1 measure brandy
champagne, chilled

1. Place the sugar cube in the
   bottom of a chilled champagne
   flute with the Angostura bitters.
2. Pour over the brandy and top off
   slowly with champagne.

APPLE CLASSIC

SERVES I

APPLE LOVERS AND CIDER MAKERS WILL PUT THIS AT THE TOP
OF THEIR LIST, BUT IT IS DEFINITELY BETTER MADE WITH SWEET
RATHER THAN DRY HARD CIDER.

½ measure gin
½ measure brandy
½ measure Calvados
cracked ice cubes
sweet hard cider
apple slice, to decorate

1. Shake the gin, brandy, and
   Calvados over cracked ice
   until frosted.
2. Strain into a chilled highball glass
   and top off with hard cider.
3. Dress with the apple slice.

BEAGLE

SERVES 1

THIS COCKTAIL FEATURES KÜMMEL, A COLORLESS LIQUEUR FLAVORED
WITH CARAWAY SEED. IT IS SAID TO HAVE ORIGINATED IN HOLLAND,
BUT NOWADAYS IS ALSO DISTILLED IN GERMANY, RUSSIA, AND
DENMARK.

cracked ice cubes
dash kümmel
dash lemon juice
2 measures brandy
1 measure cranberry juice

1. Put the cracked ice into a mixing
   glass. Add the kümmel and lemon
   juice, then pour in the brandy and
   cranberry juice.
2. Stir well to mix and strain into a
   chilled cocktail glass.

Cocktails of the Rich & Famous

Humphrey Bogart's last words may have been "I never should have switched from Scotch to Martinis," but cocktails and celebrity have been inextricably linked for as long as there has been either. The glamour, classiness, and sheer wow factor of a good cocktail makes them irresistible to the rich and famous—and to those of us eager to feel a little of that luster ourselves. Some are famous for their drinks and some for the drinks named after them.

Frank Sinatra

It was strictly Martinis for all of the Rat Pack, Hollywood's most powerful singer/actors of the 1960s—and just to show that it was Frank Sinatra's world after all, the leader of the pack was in the habit of casually dropping a jalapeño-stuffed olive into his drink and then knocking it back in one.

Marilyn Monroe

In *The Seven Year Itch*, Marilyn habitually dunks potato chips in her champagne and since her death she has lent her name to a champagne cocktail. Made with apple brandy and grenadine, it is said to taste sweet with a hidden kick!

George Clooney

The world's most eligible bachelor has made Italy his second home and while at the Venice film festival recently, he asked old friend and head barman of Venice's Hotel Cipriani to mix him a cocktail of his own creation. The result was the Buona Notte, named in honor of Clooney's film *Good Night and Good Luck*. The vodka-based drink has since found a place on the hotel's regular cocktail menu.

GINGER ROGERS
The singing and dancing foil to Fred Astaire is now also synonymous for a hugely popular, highly-drinkable cocktail made from gin, ginger ale, and mint leaves.

CHARLIE CHAPLIN
Created at the Waldorf-Astoria in honor of the actor—no stranger to a fine cocktail himself—this was one of the most popular drinks of the 1910s and 1920s. An equal mix of lime, apricot brandy, and sloe gin, it makes for a thick, sweet, deceptively gentle tipple—much like the famous Tramp himself.

WINSTON CHURCHILL
The man who saw Britain through its darkest hour did so fortified in part by his favored "highballs"—a whiskey-based drink that, in Churchill's case, was heavy on the whiskey. So heavy, in fact, that it is said that while in Africa he would add whiskey to the water to make it drinkable.

SHIRLEY TEMPLE
This nonalcoholic cocktail—a concoction of grenadine and ginger ale, topped with a cocktail cherry—dates back to the 1930s when Shirley Temple was an immensely popular child movie star. It is unclear who actually invented the cocktail (there are several claimants) but it is believed that it came into existence because she was too young to drink the cocktails enjoyed by her adult co-stars when she attended parties with them.

BRIDE'S MOTHER

1½ measures sloe gin
1 measure London gin
2½ measures grapefruit juice
½ measure sugar syrup
cracked ice cubes
lemon slice, to decorate

1. Shake the sloe gin, London gin, grapefruit juice, and sugar syrup vigorously over cracked ice until well frosted.
2. Pour into a chilled cocktail glass.
3. Dress with the lemon slice.

WEDDING BELLE

2 measures gin
2 measures Dubonnet
1 measure cherry brandy
1 measure orange juice
cracked ice cubes
orange zest strip, to decorate

1. Shake the gin, Dubonnet, cherry brandy, and orange juice over cracked ice until well frosted.
2. Strain into a chilled cocktail glass and dress with the orange zest.

Wedding Bells

Serves 1

cracked ice cubes
dash orange bitters
2 measures rye whiskey
1 measure Triple Sec
2 measures Lillet
orange zest strip, to decorate

1. Fill a mixing glass halfway with cracked ice.
    Splash orange bitters over the ice and pour in
    the rye whiskey, Triple Sec, and Lillet.
2. Stir well to mix, then strain into a chilled
    cocktail glass and dress with the orange zest.

Royal Wedding

Serves 1

1 measure Kirsch
1 measure peach brandy
1 measure orange juice
cracked ice cubes

1. Shake the Kirsch, peach brandy,
    and orange juice vigorously over
    cracked ice until well frosted.
2. Strain into a chilled glass.

DUKE

SERVES 1

A BUCK'S FIZZ—SIMPLY ORANGE JUICE AND CHAMPAGNE—IS A
GENTLY REFRESHING COCKTAIL. THE DUKE IS SIMILAR, BUT THE
ADDITION OF TRIPLE SEC UPS THE ORANGE FLAVOR, THE ALCOHOL
CONTENT, AND THE VIGOR OF THE ALARM CALL!

1 measure Triple Sec
½ measure lemon juice
½ measure orange juice
1 egg white
dash maraschino liqueur
cracked ice cubes
champagne or sparkling wine,
  chilled

1. Shake the Triple Sec, lemon
   juice, orange juice, egg white, and
   maraschino liqueur vigorously
   over cracked ice until well frosted.
2. Strain into a chilled wine
   glass and top off with chilled
   champagne.

Duchess

SERVES 1

THIS COCKTAIL INCLUDES PERNOD, WHICH IS A BRAND NAME OF A TYPE OF LIQUEUR CALLED A PASTIS. FLAVORED WITH STAR ANISE AND OTHER AROMATIC HERBS AND PLANTS, PERNOD IS PRODUCED IN FRANCE.

cracked ice cubes
1 measure Pernod
1 measure sweet vermouth
1 measure dry vermouth

1. Fill a mixing glass halfway with cracked ice. Pour over the Pernod, sweet vermouth, and dry vermouth.
2. Stir well to mix and then strain into a chilled lowball glass.

SAKETINI

SERVES 1

3 measures gin
½ measure sake
cracked ice cubes
lemon zest strip, to decorate

1. Shake the gin and sake vigorously over
   cracked ice until well frosted.
2. Strain into a chilled cocktail glass and dress
   with the lemon zest.

RAFFLES KNOCKOUT

SERVES 1

1 measure Triple Sec
1 measure Kirsch
dash lemon juice
cracked ice cubes
cocktail cherries and lemon slice, to decorate

1. Shake the Triple Sec, Kirsch, and lemon juice
   vigorously over cracked ice until well frosted.
2. Strain into a chilled cocktail glass.
3. Dress with the cocktail cherries and
   lemon slice.

HALLEY'S COMFORT

cracked ice cubes
2 measures Southern Comfort
2 measures peach schnapps
sparkling water
lemon slice, to decorate

1. Fill a chilled lowball glass with cracked ice.
2. Pour the Southern Comfort and peach schnapps over the ice and top off with sparkling water.
3. Stir gently and dress with the lemon slice.

MILLIONAIRE MIX

1 measure rye whiskey
½ measure grenadine
½ measure curaçao
½ egg white
cracked ice cubes
dash Pernod

1. Shake the rye whiskey, grenadine, curaçao, and egg white over cracked ice.
2. Strain into a wine glass and, at the last minute, add the Pernod.

ROLLS-ROYCE

SERVES 1

JUST LIKE THE LUXURY AUTOMOBILE FOR WHICH IT IS NAMED, THIS COCKTAIL IS SYNONYMOUS WITH OPULENCE AND SPLENDOR. THE FRENCH LIQUEUR BÉNÉDICTINE, FLAVORED WITH HERBS, SPICES, AND HONEY, IS A KEY INGREDIENT.

cracked ice cubes
3 measures gin
1 measure dry vermouth
1 measure sweet vermouth
¼ tsp Bénédictine

1. Fill a mixing glass with cracked ice.
2. Pour over the gin, dry vermouth, sweet vermouth, and Bénédictine.
3. Stir well to mix and then strain into a chilled cocktail glass.

Golden Cadillac

Serves 1

This indulgent cocktail was invented in New York during the 1950s to celebrate the Cadillac's 50th anniversary. The yellow color comes from the Italian Galliano liqueur.

lemon wedge
superfine sugar
1 measure Triple Sec
1 measure Galliano
1 measure light cream
cracked ice cubes

1. Rub the rim of a chilled cocktail glass with the lemon wedge, then dip into a saucer of sugar to frost.
2. Shake the Triple Sec, Galliano, and light cream vigorously over cracked ice until well frosted.
3. Strain into the cocktail glass.

Rosita

Serves 1

cracked ice cubes
2 measures Campari
2 measures white tequila
½ measure dry vermouth
½ measure sweet vermouth
lime zest strip, to decorate

1. Fill a mixing glass with cracked ice.
2. Pour over the Campari, tequila, dry vermouth, and sweet vermouth.
3. Stir well to mix, then strain into a chilled lowball glass.
4. Dress with the lime zest.

Chica Chica

Serves 1

2 measures raspberry vodka
1 measure Chambéry (a type of white vermouth)
2 measures cranberry and raspberry juice
crushed ice cubes
1 measure apple juice
lemon-flavored soda pop
apple slice, to decorate

1. Mix the raspberry vodka, Chambéry, cranberry and raspberry juice, and crushed ice together in a chilled highball glass.
2. Stir in the apple juice and top off with soda pop.
3. Dress with the apple slice.

Star Daisy

2 measures gin
1½ measures apple brandy
1½ measures lemon juice
1 tsp sugar syrup
½ tsp Triple Sec
cracked ice cubes
club soda

1. Shake the gin, apple brandy, lemon juice, sugar syrup, and Triple Sec vigorously over cracked ice until well frosted.
2. Pour into a chilled lowball glass and top off with club soda.

Walking Zombie

Serves 1

1 measure white rum
1 measure golden rum
1 measure dark rum
1 measure apricot brandy
1 measure lime juice
1 measure pineapple juice
1 tsp sugar syrup
cracked ice cubes
orange and lime slices, to decorate

1. Shake the white rum, golden rum, dark rum, apricot brandy, lime juice, pineapple juice, and sugar syrup vigorously over cracked ice until frosted.
2. Fill a chilled highball glass halfway with cracked ice and strain over the cocktail.
3. Dress with the orange and lime slices.

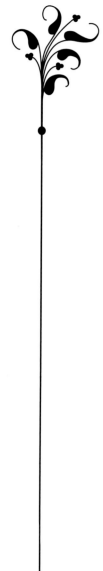

BLANCHE

PERNOD IS A CLEAR LIQUEUR THAT TURNS CLOUDY WHEN MIXED WITH WATER OR ICE. THIS MILKY WHITE COLOR GIVES THIS CLASSY COCKTAIL ITS NAME.

1 measure Pernod
1 measure Triple Sec
½ measure clear curaçao
cracked ice cubes

1. Shake the Pernod, Triple Sec, and clear curaçao vigorously over cracked ice until well frosted.
2. Strain into a chilled cocktail glass.

SEVENTH HEAVEN

SERVES 1

WE GUARANTEE THAT YOU'LL BE WALKING ON AIR AFTER TASTING
THIS DELICIOUS DRINK, WHICH IS A CLASSIC COMBINATION OF GIN,
MARASCHINO LIQUEUR, AND GRAPEFRUIT JUICE SHAKEN OVER ICE.

2 measures gin
½ measure maraschino liqueur
½ measure grapefruit juice
cracked ice cubes
fresh mint sprig, to decorate

1. Shake the gin, maraschino liqueur,
    and grapefruit juice vigorously
    over cracked ice until well frosted.
2. Strain into a chilled cocktail glass
    and dress with the mint sprig.

PARTY STARTERS

TEQUILA SLAMMER

SERVES 1

SLAMMERS ARE ALSO KNOWN AS SHOOTERS. THE IDEA IS THAT YOU POUR THE INGREDIENTS DIRECTLY INTO THE GLASS, WITHOUT STIRRING. COVER THE GLASS WITH ONE HAND, SLAM IT ONTO A TABLE TO MIX, AND DRINK THE COCKTAIL DOWN IN ONE!

1 measure white tequila, chilled
1 measure lemon juice
sparkling wine, chilled

1. Put the tequila and lemon juice into a chilled glass.
2. Top off with sparkling wine.
3. Cover the glass with your hand and slam.

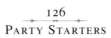

Alabama Slammer

Serves 1

THIS POTENT COCKTAIL WAS CREATED AT THE UNIVERSITY OF
ALABAMA IN THE 1970S. SMALL, BUT PERFECTLY PROPORTIONED, IT
IS A SHOOTER WITH A REAL KICK!

1 measure Southern Comfort
1 measure amaretto
½ measure sloe gin
cracked ice cubes
½ tsp lemon juice

1. Pour the Southern Comfort,
   amaretto, and sloe gin over
   cracked ice in a mixing glass
   and stir.
2. Strain into a chilled shot glass and
   add the lemon juice.

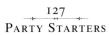

B-52

1 measure dark crème de cacao, chilled
1 measure Baileys Irish Cream, chilled
1 measure Grand Marnier, chilled

1. Pour the dark crème de cacao into a chilled shot glass.
2. With a steady hand, gently pour in the chilled Baileys Irish Cream to make a second layer, then gently pour in the chilled Grand Marnier.
3. Cover the glass with your hand and slam.

CORDLESS SCREWDRIVER

orange wedges
granulated sugar
2 measures vodka, chilled

1. Rub the rim of a shot glass with an orange wedge, then dip in a saucer of sugar to frost.
2. Pour the chilled vodka into the glass.
3. Dip an orange wedge into the sugar.
4. Down the vodka in one gulp and suck on the orange.

COWBOY

3 measures rye whiskey
2 tbsp half-and-half
cracked ice cubes

1. Pour the whiskey and half-and-half over cracked ice and shake vigorously until well frosted.
2. Strain into a chilled glass.

POUSSE-CAFÉ

¼ measure grenadine, chilled
¼ measure crème de menthe, chilled
¼ measure Galliano, chilled
¼ measure kümmel, chilled
¼ measure brandy, chilled

1. Carefully pour the liqueurs, one by one, over the back of a spoon into a chilled shot or pousse-café glass.
2. Leave for a few minutes to settle.

RUSSIAN DOUBLE

SERVES 1

VODKA AND SCHNAPPS ARE BOTH VERY POPULAR DRINKS IN RUSSIA.
HOWEVER, THEY ARE BOTH VERY STRONG, SO THIS SHOOTER NEEDS
TO BE HANDLED WITH CARE!

1 measure red vodka, chilled
lemon or orange zest strips
1 measure lemon vodka or
  schnapps, chilled

I. Layer the ingredients carefully
in a chilled shot glass, putting
the lemon zest in the first layer.
Drink immediately.

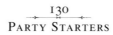

IRISH STINGER

SERVES 1

A SHORT DRINK WITH A STING IN ITS TAIL! THE CLASSIC STINGER
COCKTAIL IS A MIXTURE OF BRANDY AND WHITE CRÈME DE
MENTHE—THIS IS ITS IRISH COUSIN.

1 measure Baileys Irish Cream
1 measure white crème de
  menthe
cracked ice cubes

1. Shake the Baileys Irish Cream and
white crème de menthe vigorously
over cracked ice until well frosted.
2. Strain into a chilled shot or
lowball glass.

Drinking Games

Although most cocktails are intended to be served in a civilized, cultured atmosphere, it doesn't do any harm to occasionally cut loose and have a little fun. Drinking games may evoke memories of student parties and over-inebriated summer vacations, but there are a few you can play that manage to be both uproarious fun and shouldn't hit you too hard the next morning!

I Have Never...

For this game, everyone starts with a full glass in front of them (a bottle for top-ups should be close by!). The players take turns to speak and on their turn each must say a true statement about themselves beginning with the words: "I have never..."

Whoever the statement does not apply to has to drink. For example, if the statement is "I have never seen *Casablanca*," then every player who has seen the film should down their shot.

If, however, the statement does not apply to anyone (i.e. none of the other players has seen *Casablanca* either), then the person who made the statement should drink instead.

The idea is to get as many of your fellow players drinking as possible, while at the same time learning some juicy secrets!

Finger It

Best played with champagne in a saucer-shaped coupe (or if you prefer, a Martini in a traditional glass). Everyone places one finger around the rim of the glass. One player calls out a prediction for how many fingers will be left on the glass and, as the number is called out, everyone either removes or leaves their finger where it is.

If the player has guessed correctly, they drop out of the circle (if not, they stay in), everyone replaces their fingers on the rim of the glass, and the next player calls out a number. The game continues until only one person is left—and they must down the drink.

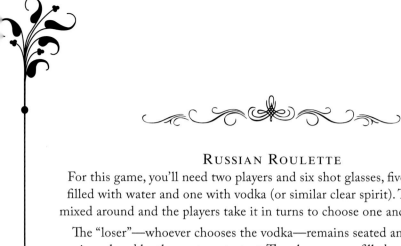

Russian Roulette

For this game, you'll need two players and six shot glasses, five of which are filled with water and one with vodka (or similar clear spirit). The glasses are mixed around and the players take it in turns to choose one and knock it back.

The "loser"—whoever chooses the vodka—remains seated and the winner is replaced by the next contestant. The glasses are refilled and the game begins again.

Caution should be exercised with this one—an unlucky run can see a player becoming drunk very quickly!

Tricolor

Serves 1

1 measure maraschino liqueur, chilled
1 measure green crème de menthe, chilled
1 measure Baileys Irish Cream, chilled

1. Pour the chilled maraschino liqueur into a chilled shot glass.
2. With a steady hand, pour in the chilled crème de menthe over the back of a spoon to make a second layer.
3. For the final layer, repeat with the chilled Baileys Irish Cream.

Tornado

Serves 1

1 measure peach or other favorite schnapps, chilled
1 measure black sambuca, chilled

1. Pour the schnapps into a chilled shot glass.
2. Gently pour in the sambuca over the back of a spoon.
3. Leave for a few minutes to settle and separate.

TOFFEE SPLIT

crushed ice cubes
2 measures Drambuie
1 measure toffee liqueur, chilled

1. Fill a shot glass with crushed ice.
2. Pour in the Drambuie, then pour the toffee liqueur over the back of a spoon to make a layer on top.

NUCLEAR FALLOUT

1 tsp framboise liqueur, chilled
¼ measure maraschino liqueur, chilled
¼ measure yellow Chartreuse, chilled
¼ measure Cointreau, chilled
½ measure blue curaçao, chilled

1. Carefully pour the framboise, maraschino liqueur, Chartreuse, and Cointreau, one by one, over the back of a spoon into a chilled shot or pousse-café glass.
2. Finally, pour in the curaçao and wait for the fallout!

WHITE DIAMOND FRAPPÉ

SERVES 1

THIS IS A CRAZY COMBINATION OF LIQUEURS, BUT IT WORKS WELL
ONCE YOU'VE ADDED THE LEMON. ADDING EXTRA CRUSHED ICE AT
THE LAST MINUTE BRINGS OUT ALL THE SEPARATE FLAVORS.

¼ measure peppermint schnapps
¼ measure white crème de cacao
¼ measure anise liqueur
¼ measure lemon juice
cracked and crushed ice cubes

1. Shake all the liquid ingredients
   over cracked ice until frosted.
2. Strain into a chilled shot glass
   and add a small spoonful of
   crushed ice.

PEACH FLOYD

SERVES 1

SHOTS LOOK STUNNING IN THE RIGHT TYPE OF GLASS, BUT BECAUSE
THEY ARE FOR DRINKING DOWN IN ONE, KEEP THEM SMALL AND
HAVE EVERYTHING REALLY WELL CHILLED.

1 measure peach schnapps,
  chilled
1 measure vodka, chilled
1 measure white cranberry and
  peach juice, chilled
1 measure cranberry juice, chilled
cracked ice cubes

1. Stir all the liquid ingredients
   together over cracked ice.
2. Strain into an iced shot glass.

Voodoo

½ measure Kahlúa, chilled
½ measure Malibu, chilled
½ measure butterscotch schnapps, chilled
1 measure milk, chilled

1. Pour the Kahlúa, Malibu, schnapps, and milk into a chilled shot glass and stir well.

Depth Charge

1 measure gin
1 measure Lillet
2 dashes Pernod
cracked ice cubes

1. Shake all the liquid ingredients over cracked ice until well frosted.
2. Strain into a chilled shot glass.

SANGRITA

SERVES 16

2½ cups tomato juice
1¼ cups orange juice
½ cup lime juice
1 jalapeño chile, seeded and finely chopped
1 tbsp Worcestershire sauce
1 tbsp Tabasco sauce
celery salt and ground white pepper
3¼ cups tequila, chilled

1. Pour the tomato juice, orange juice, and lime juice into a large pitcher and stir in the chile, Worcestershire sauce, and Tabasco sauce. Season with celery salt and white pepper, then chill for at least 1 hour.
2. To serve, pour a measure of tequila into a chilled shot glass and a measure of sangrita into a second shot glass. Drink the tequila in a single gulp, then chase with the sangrita.

FIRELIGHTER

SERVES 1

1 measure absinthe, iced
1 measure lime cordial, iced
cracked ice cubes

1. Shake the absinthe and lime cordial vigorously over cracked ice until well frosted.
2. Strain into an iced shot glass.

BLOODY BRAIN

SERVES 1

THIS IS A RARE INSTANCE OF A COCKTAIL THAT IS DELIBERATELY
INTENDED TO LOOK HORRID, RATHER THAN TEMPTING, AND WAS
PROBABLY INVENTED TO DRINK AT HALLOWEEN.

1 measure peach schnapps,
  chilled
1 tsp Baileys Irish Cream, chilled
½ tsp grenadine, chilled

1. Pour the peach schnapps into a
   shot glass, then carefully pour the
   Baileys Irish Cream on top.
2. Finally, pour in the grenadine.

CAPUCINE

SERVES 1

CHILLED LIQUEURS ARE OFTEN SERVED OVER FINELY CRUSHED ICE
AS A FRAPPÉ. THIS VERSION IS TIERED FOR TWICE THE EFFECT.

crushed ice cubes
1 measure blue curaçao, chilled
1 measure Parfait Amour, chilled

1. Fill a shot glass with crushed ice.
2. Pour in the curaçao slowly and then carefully add the Parfait Amour.

Angel's Delight

Serves 1

½ measure grenadine, chilled
½ measure Triple Sec, chilled
½ measure sloe gin, chilled
½ measure light cream, chilled

1. Pour the grenadine into a chilled shot or pousse-café glass, then, with a steady hand, pour in the Triple Sec to make a second layer.
2. Add the sloe gin to make a third layer and, finally, add the cream to float on top.

Anouchka

Serves 1

1 measure vodka, chilled
dash black sambuca
dash crème de mure
blackberries, to decorate

1. Pour the vodka into a chilled shot glass.
2. Add the sambuca and crème de mure.
3. Dress with the blackberries.

SPUTNIK

SERVES 1

1 measure vodka
1 measure light cream
1 tsp maraschino liqueur
cracked ice cubes
cocktail cherry, to decorate

1. Shake all the liquid ingredients vigorously over cracked ice and strain into a chilled shot glass.
2. Dress with the cocktail cherry.

MOON LANDING

SERVES 1

1 measure vodka
1 measure Tia Maria
1 measure amaretto
1 measure Baileys Irish Cream
cracked ice cubes

1. Shake the vodka, Tia Maria, amaretto, and Baileys Irish Cream over cracked ice until well frosted.
2. Strain into a chilled shot glass.

Whiskey Gelatin Shot

Serves 8

A NEW TWIST ON A CLASSIC COCKTAIL FOR A NEW GENERATION OF
COCKTAIL DRINKERS, BUT BE CAREFUL TO KEEP CHILDREN AWAY
FROM THE REFRIGERATOR.

1 package lemon gelatin
1 cup hot water
¾–1 cup bourbon whiskey

1. Place the gelatin in a large heatproof measuring cup or pitcher. Pour in the hot water and stir until the gelatin has dissolved. Let cool, then stir in the bourbon to make the mixture up to 2 cups.

2. Divide among 8 shot glasses and chill until set.

Cosmo Gelatin Shot

Serves 8

This gelatin shot cocktail pays homage to the original Cosmopolitan cocktail. It is not essential to frost the glasses with salt but it does look attractive.

½ lime, cut into wedges
2 tbsp fine salt
1 package lime gelatin
¾ cup hot water
4 tbsp Cointreau
¾ cup vodka
¾ cup cranberry juice

1. Rub the rims of 8 shot glasses with the lime wedges, then dip in the salt to frost.
2. Place the gelatin in a large heatproof measuring cup or pitcher. Pour in the hot water and stir until the gelatin has dissolved. Let cool, then stir in the Cointreau, vodka, and cranberry juice.
3. Divide among the prepared shot glasses and chill until set.

AFTER DINNER

MUDSLIDE

SERVES I

DESPITE ITS OMINOUS-SOUNDING NAME, THIS IS A RICHLY FLAVORED
CREAMY CONCOCTION THAT IS DELICIOUS WHATEVER THE WEATHER
AND EASILY SLIDES DOWN THE THROAT.

1½ measures Kahlúa
1½ measures Baileys Irish Cream
1½ measures vodka
cracked ice cubes

1. Shake the Kahlúa, Baileys Irish
   Cream, and vodka vigorously over
   cracked ice until well frosted.
2. Strain into a chilled glass.

BLACK RUSSIAN

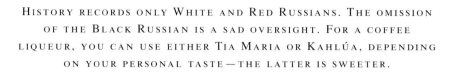

HISTORY RECORDS ONLY WHITE AND RED RUSSIANS. THE OMISSION OF THE BLACK RUSSIAN IS A SAD OVERSIGHT. FOR A COFFEE LIQUEUR, YOU CAN USE EITHER TIA MARIA OR KAHLÚA, DEPENDING ON YOUR PERSONAL TASTE — THE LATTER IS SWEETER.

cracked ice cubes
2 measures vodka
1 measure coffee liqueur

1. Fill a lowball glass halfway with cracked ice.
2. Pour over the vodka and coffee liqueur and stir to mix.

Pink Whiskers

2 measures apricot brandy
1 measure dry vermouth
2 measures orange juice
dash grenadine
cracked ice cubes

1. Shake the apricot brandy, dry vermouth, orange juice, and grenadine vigorously over cracked ice until well frosted.
2. Strain into a chilled cocktail glass.

Port Wine Cobbler

1 tsp superfine sugar
2 measures sparkling water
cracked ice cubes
3 measures ruby port
orange slice and cocktail cherry, to decorate

1. Put the sugar into a chilled wine glass and add the sparkling water. Stir until the sugar has dissolved.
2. Fill the glass with cracked ice and pour in the ruby port.
3. Dress with the orange slice and cocktail cherry.

FLYING SCOTSMAN

SERVES 1

4–6 ice cubes, crushed
dash Angostura bitters
2 measures Scotch whisky
1 measure sweet vermouth
¼ tsp sugar syrup

1. Put the crushed ice into a blender, and add the Angostura bitters, Scotch whisky, sweet vermouth, and sugar syrup.
2. Blend until slushy and pour into a chilled lowball glass.

WHITE SPIDER

SERVES 1

1 measure vodka
1 measure white crème de menthe
cracked ice cubes

1. Pour the vodka and white crème de menthe over cracked ice in a mixing glass.
2. Stir well and strain into a chilled cocktail glass.

LEAP YEAR

SERVES 1

CELEBRATE FEBRUARY 29TH IN STYLE WITH THIS CLASSIC COCKTAIL,
WHICH IS AN ADAPTATION OF THE RECIPE CREATED BY HARRY
CRADDOCK FOR THE 1928 LEAP YEAR CELEBRATIONS AT THE SAVOY
HOTEL, LONDON.

2 measures gin
½ measure Grand Marnier
½ measure sweet vermouth
½ tsp lemon juice
cracked ice cubes

1. Shake the gin, Grand Marnier, sweet vermouth, and lemon juice vigorously over cracked ice until well frosted.
2. Strain into a chilled cocktail glass.

SOUTHERN PEACH

SERVES 1

THE WHISKEY-BASED LIQUEUR SOUTHERN COMFORT HAS A NATURAL
AFFINITY WITH PEACHES. PERFECT FOR DESSERT, THIS IS AN
ALCOHOLIC TAKE ON PEACHES AND CREAM.

1 measure Southern Comfort
1 measure peach brandy
1 measure light cream
dash Angostura bitters
cracked ice cubes
peach slice, to decorate

1. Shake the Southern Comfort,
   peach brandy, cream, and
   Angostura bitters vigorously over
   cracked ice until well frosted.
2. Strain into a chilled glass and
   dress with the peach slice.

Amaretto Stinger

Serves 1

2 measures amaretto
1 measure white crème de menthe
cracked ice cubes

1. Shake the amaretto and crème de menthe vigorously over cracked ice until well frosted.
2. Strain into a chilled shot glass.

Banana Slip

Serves 1

1 measure crème de banane, chilled
1 measure Baileys Irish Cream, chilled

1. Pour the chilled crème de banane into a chilled shot glass.
2. With a steady hand, gently pour in the chilled Baileys Irish Cream to make a second layer.

DANDY

½ measure rye whiskey
½ measure Dubonnet
dash Angostura bitters
3 dashes crème de cassis
cracked ice cubes
frozen strawberry, to decorate

1. Pour the whiskey, Dubonnet, Angostura bitters, and crème de cassis into a mixing glass with cracked ice.
2. Stir well to mix and then strain into a chilled shot glass.
3. Dress with the frozen strawberry.

JEALOUSY

SERVES I

1 tsp white crème de menthe
1–2 tbsp heavy cream
2 measures coffee or chocolate liqueur
chocolate matchsticks, to serve

1. Gently beat the crème de menthe into the cream until thick.
2. Pour the coffee liqueur into a chilled shot glass and carefully spoon on the whipped flavored cream.
3. Serve with the chocolate matchsticks.

RATTLESNAKE

SERVES 1

THIS POTENT LAYERED DRINK IS NAMED FOR ITS RESEMBLANCE TO A
VENOMOUS SNAKE'S STRIPED TAIL. NEVER MIND ITS RATTLE, WATCH
OUT FOR ITS BITE!

1 measure dark crème de cacao, chilled

1 measure Baileys Irish Cream, chilled

1 measure Kahlúa, chilled

1. Pour the chilled crème de cacao into a chilled shot glass.
2. With a steady hand, gently pour in the chilled Baileys Irish Cream over the back of a spoon to make a second layer.
3. For the final layer, repeat with the chilled Kahlúa.

NAPOLEON'S NIGHTCAP

SERVES I

INSTEAD OF HOT CHOCOLATE, THE EMPEROR OF FRANCE APPARENTLY
FAVORED CHOCOLATE-LACED BRANDY WITH A HINT OF BANANA.
DARING AND EXTRAVAGANT, LIKE THE MAN HIMSELF!

1¼ measures cognac
1 measure dark crème de cacao
¼ measure crème de banane
cracked ice cubes
1 tbsp heavy cream

1. Stir the cognac, crème de cacao, and crème de banane in a mixing glass with cracked ice.
2. Strain into a chilled cocktail glass and spoon on a layer of cream.

Hangover Cures

Cocktails are, by definition, a potent alcoholic mix and it can be easy to be tempted into having just one more than your body is happy with. Of course, they are better enjoyed in moderation—cocktails are the perfect example of the superiority of quality over quantity—but, unfortunately, all of us overindulge once in a while.

Eating before you drink helps to avoid a hangover the next day, as does alternating your drinks with (non-fizzy) water. A glass of orange juice before bed can help your liver to speed up the metabolism of the alcohol, too.

If all else fails, try the following cures—we've graded them according to the severity of the morning after.

The mild hangover (pain level 3–5/10)
Eat mineral-rich foods—fried food is traditional, but pickles or canned fish do the job better. The Polish—who know a thing or two about spirits—swear by pickle juice.

Get some exercise. Assuming you can move at all, sweating the badness out of your body can work—just remember to drink lots of water.

The seriously uncomfortable hangover (pain level 5–7/10)
Sleep, water, and fruit juice are your best friends. Keep yourself hydrated, load up on vitamin C, and spend an extra couple of hours in bed.

Take a long shower, alternating between hot and cold water. The shock should give your body something else to worry about.

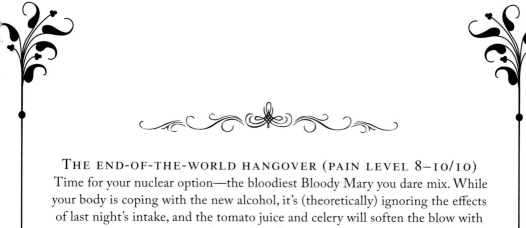

THE END-OF-THE-WORLD HANGOVER (PAIN LEVEL 8–10/10)

Time for your nuclear option—the bloodiest Bloody Mary you dare mix. While your body is coping with the new alcohol, it's (theoretically) ignoring the effects of last night's intake, and the tomato juice and celery will soften the blow with plenty of good vitamins.

Whatever you do, avoid caffeine (dehydration plus more dehydration equals worse hangover) and, believe it or not, painkillers are also a bad idea. Aspirin and ibuprofen can irritate a delicate stomach, and paracetamol only gives your liver more work to do.

And most importantly, take it a bit easier next time!

Fifth Avenue

re dark crème de cacao, chilled
re apricot brandy, chilled
re heavy cream

r the chilled crème de cacao into a chilled
  or pousse-café glass.
fully pour in the apricot brandy over the
  of a spoon to make a second layer.
lly, float the cream on top.

African Mint

¾ measure green crème de menthe, chilled
¾ measure Amarula, chilled

1. Pour the crème de menthe into a chilled shot
   glass, saving a few drops.
2. Pour the Amarula slowly over the back of a
   spoon so that it forms a separate layer.
3. Drizzle the remaining drops of crème de
   menthe over the creamy liqueur to finish.

AFTER FIVE

½ measure peppermint schnapps, chilled
1 measure Kahlúa, chilled
1 tbsp Baileys Irish Cream, chilled

1. Pour the peppermint schnapps into a chilled shot or pousse-café glass.
2. Carefully pour in the Kahlúa over the back of a spoon to make a second layer.
3. Finally, float the Baileys Irish Cream on top.

PEPPERMINT PATTY

1 measure crème de cacao
1 measure crème de menthe
cracked ice cubes

1. Shake the crème de cacao and crème de menthe vigorously over cracked ice until well frosted.
2. Strain into a chilled shot glass.

Irish Cow

SERVES 1

MILK-BASED COCKTAILS ARE THE PERFECT AFTER-DINNER TIPPLE
OR NIGHTCAP. THIS ONE USES IRISH WHISKEY BUT YOU COULD TRY
USING A CREAM LIQUEUR, SUCH AS BAILEYS IRISH CREAM, INSTEAD.

1 cup milk
2 measures Irish whiskey
1 tsp superfine sugar

1. Heat the milk in a small pan to just below boiling point.
2. Remove from the heat and pour into a warmed heatproof glass or mug.
3. Add the Irish whiskey and sugar, and stir until the sugar has dissolved.

BOURBON MILK PUNCH

SERVES I

THIS TEMPTING DRINK IS A DELIGHTFUL ALTERNATIVE TO EGGNOG
FOR THE HOLIDAY SEASON. TO MAKE IT EXTRA-LUXURIOUS, USE
HALF-AND-HALF IN PLACE OF THE MILK.

2 measures bourbon whiskey
3 measures milk
1 tsp honey
dash vanilla extract
cracked ice cubes
freshly grated nutmeg,
   for sprinkling

1. Shake the bourbon, milk, honey,
and vanilla extract over cracked ice
until well frosted.
2. Strain into a chilled lowball glass
and sprinkle with the grated
nutmeg.

Hungarian Coffee

Serves 1

2 measures brandy
sugar
freshly made strong black coffee
1 tbsp grated chocolate
whipped cream
cinnamon stick, to decorate

1. Put the brandy into a warmed heatproof glass and add sugar to taste.
2. Pour in the coffee and grated chocolate, and stir.
3. When the sugar has completely dissolved and the chocolate has melted, top with the whipped cream and dress with the cinnamon stick.
4. Don't stir—drink the coffee through the cream.

Irish Coffee

Serves 1

2 measures Irish whiskey
sugar
freshly made strong black coffee
2 measures heavy cream

1. Put the whiskey into a warmed heatproof glass and add sugar to taste.
2. Pour in the coffee and stir.
3. When the sugar has completely dissolved, pour in the cream very slowly over the back of a spoon so that it floats on top.
4. Don't stir—drink the coffee through the cream.

Amaretto Coffee

1½ measures amaretto
sugar
freshly made strong black coffee
1–2 tbsp heavy cream

1. Put the amaretto into a warmed heatproof glass and add sugar to taste.
2. Pour in the coffee and stir.
3. When the sugar has completely dissolved, pour in the cream very slowly over the back of a spoon so that it floats on top.
4. Don't stir—drink the coffee through the cream.

Espresso Galliano

2 measures Galliano
sugar
freshly made strong black coffee
splash orange or lemon juice
orange zest strip, to decorate

1. Put the Galliano into a warmed heatproof glass and add sugar to taste.
2. Pour in the coffee and orange juice, and stir until the sugar has completely dissolved.
3. Dress with the orange zest.

Hot Brandy Chocolate

Serves 4

BRANDY AND CHOCOLATE CERTAINLY HAVE A NATURAL AFFINITY, AS THIS DELICIOUS DRINK DEMONSTRATES. IT'S A WARMING AND COMFORTING BEVERAGE FOR A COLD WINTER'S EVENING.

5 cups milk
4 oz/115 g semisweet chocolate, broken into pieces
2 tbsp sugar
4 measures brandy
6 tbsp whipped cream
freshly grated nutmeg or unsweetened cocoa, for sprinkling

1. Heat the milk in a small pan to just below boiling point.
2. Add the chocolate and sugar, and stir over low heat until the chocolate has melted.
3. Pour into 4 warmed heatproof glasses, then pour 1 measure of the brandy over the back of a spoon on top of each.
4. Add the whipped cream and sprinkle over the grated nutmeg.

MULLED WINE

SERVES 4

THIS DRINK IS CHRISTMAS IN A GLASS! MAKE SURE TO WARM IT
THROUGH GENTLY AND GIVE THE SPICES TIME TO INFUSE THE WINE
WITH THEIR AROMATIC FLAVORS.

3 cups red wine
2 measures sherry
8 cloves
1 cinnamon stick
½ tsp ground allspice
2 tbsp honey
1 orange, cut into wedges
1 lemon, cut into wedges

1. Put the wine, sherry, cloves, cinnamon, allspice, and honey into a pan. Warm over low heat, stirring, until just starting to simmer, but do not let it boil.
2. Remove from the heat and pour through a strainer. Discard the cloves and cinnamon stick.
3. Return the pan to the heat with the orange and lemon wedges and warm gently. Pour into 4 warmed heatproof glasses.

Non-alcoholic

SHIRLEY TEMPLE

SERVES I

THIS IS ONE OF THE MOST FAMOUS OF THE CLASSIC NONALCOHOLIC
COCKTAILS AND DATES TO THE 1930S WHEN SHIRLEY TEMPLE WAS A
HUGELY POPULAR CHILD MOVIE STAR.

2 measures lemon juice
½ measure grenadine
½ measure sugar syrup
cracked ice cubes
ginger ale
orange slice, to decorate

1. Shake the lemon juice, grenadine, and sugar syrup vigorously over cracked ice until well frosted.
2. Fill a chilled highball glass halfway with cracked ice and strain the liquid into it.
3. Top off with ginger ale and dress with the orange slice.

RED APPLE SUNSET

SERVES 1

SWEET AND REFRESHING, THIS IS THE IDEAL COCKTAIL TO ENJOY AS
YOU WATCH THE SUN SINK BENEATH THE HORIZON. THE ADDITION
OF GRENADINE GIVES IT ITS PRETTY PINK COLOR.

2 measures apple juice
2 measures grapefruit juice
dash grenadine
cracked ice cubes

1. Shake the apple juice, grapefruit juice, and grenadine over cracked ice until well frosted.
2. Strain into a chilled cocktail glass.

SALTY PUPPY

granulated sugar
coarse salt
lime wedge
cracked ice cubes
½ measure lime juice
grapefruit juice

1. Mix equal quantities of the sugar and salt together on a saucer. Rub the rim of a chilled highball glass with the lime wedge and dip it into the sugar-and-salt mixture to frost.
2. Fill the glass with cracked ice and add the lime juice. Top off with grapefruit juice.

MINI COLADA

6 measures milk
4 measures pineapple juice
3 measures coconut cream
cracked ice cubes
pineapple cubes, pineapple leaf,
    and cocktail cherry, to decorate

1. Shake the milk, pineapple juice, and coconut cream vigorously over cracked ice until well frosted.
2. Fill a highball glass halfway with cracked ice and strain the liquid into it.
3. Dress with the pineapple cubes, pineapple leaf, and cocktail cherry.

HEAVENLY DAYS

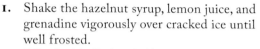

SERVES I

2 measures hazelnut syrup
2 measures lemon juice
1 tsp grenadine
cracked ice cubes
sparkling water
lime slice and star fruit slice,
    to decorate

1. Shake the hazelnut syrup, lemon juice, and
   grenadine vigorously over cracked ice until
   well frosted.
2. Fill a highball glass halfway with cracked ice
   and strain the liquid into it.
3. Top off with sparkling water. Stir gently and
   dress with the lime and star fruit slices.

BITE OF THE APPLE

SERVES I

crushed ice cubes
5 measures apple juice
1 measure lime juice
½ tsp orgeat syrup
1 tbsp applesauce or apple puree
ground cinnamon, for sprinkling

1. In a blender, process the crushed
   ice with the apple juice, lime juice,
   orgeat syrup, and applesauce until
   smooth.
2. Pour into a chilled lowball glass and
   sprinkle with the cinnamon.

FAUX KIR ROYALE

SERVES 1

A NONALCOHOLIC VERSION OF THE CLASSIC CHAMPAGNE COCKTAIL, THIS DRINK IS JUST AS COLORFUL AND TASTY. IT IS THE PERFECT DRINK FOR SUMMER PARTIES IN THE GARDEN.

cracked ice cubes
1½ measures raspberry syrup
sparkling apple juice, chilled

1. Put the cracked ice into a mixing glass and pour the raspberry syrup over it.
2. Stir well to mix, then pour into a chilled wine glass.
3. Top off with chilled sparkling apple juice and stir.

MAIDENLY MIMOSA

SERVES 2

THE CLASSIC MIMOSA COCKTAIL IS A COMBINATION OF ORANGE JUICE
AND SPARKLING WINE THAT IS TRADITIONALLY SERVED FOR BRUNCH
AND AT WEDDINGS. THIS ALCOHOL-FREE VERSION IS IDEAL FOR
YOUNGER GUESTS AND NON-DRINKERS.

¾ cup orange juice
¾ cup sparkling white grape juice

1. Divide the orange juice between 2 chilled champagne flutes.
2. Top off with sparkling grape juice.

Cherry Kiss

cracked ice cubes
2 tbsp cherry syrup
sparkling water
fresh cherries, to decorate

1. Fill 2 highball glasses with cracked ice and pour over the cherry syrup.
2. Top off with sparkling water and dress with the cherries.

Knicks Victory Cooler

cracked ice cubes
2 measures apricot juice
raspberry juice
orange zest strip and raspberries, to decorate

1. Fill a chilled highball glass halfway with cracked ice.
2. Pour in the apricot juice, top off with raspberry juice, and stir gently.
3. Dress with the orange zest and raspberries.

Cool Collins

6 fresh mint leaves
1 tsp superfine sugar
2 measures lemon juice
cracked ice cubes
sparkling water
fresh mint sprig and lemon slice,
  to decorate

1. Put the mint leaves into a chilled Collins glass
   and add the sugar and lemon juice. Mash the
   leaves with a muddler or spoon until the sugar
   has dissolved.
2. Fill the glass with cracked ice and top off with
   sparkling water.
3. Stir gently and dress with the mint sprig and
   lemon slice.

Baby Bellini

2 measures peach juice
1 measure lemon juice
sparkling apple juice

1. Pour the peach juice and lemon
   juice into a chilled champagne
   flute and stir well.
2. Top off with sparkling apple juice and
   stir again.

PROHIBITION PUNCH

SERVES 25

ALTHOUGH MOST PUNCHES TEND TO BE HEAVY ON THE ALCOHOL,
THIS ONE IS AN EXCEPTION TO THAT RULE. ITS UNUSUAL
PRESENTATION GIVES IT A PLAYFUL APPEARANCE THAT WILL APPEAL
TO CHILDREN.

3¾ cups apple juice
1½ cups lemon juice
½ cup sugar syrup
cracked ice cubes
9½ cups ginger ale
orange slices, to decorate

1. Pour the apple juice, lemon juice, and sugar syrup into a large pitcher.
2. Add the cracked ice and ginger ale. Stir gently to mix.
3. Pour into chilled highball or lowball glasses and dress with the orange slices.

FUZZY PEG

SERVES I

THIS CLASSIC ICE CREAM SODA IS A CHILD'S DELIGHT, BOTH IN TASTE AND ITS INCREDIBLE APPEARANCE. IT COULD BE MADE USING OTHER FLAVORS OF SODA, ALTHOUGH IT'S BEST TO STICK WITH VANILLA ICE CREAM.

2 scoops vanilla ice cream
1 measure lime or lemon cordial
cracked ice cubes
cola

1. In a blender, process the ice cream and lime cordial until smooth.
2. Fill a highball glass with cracked ice and pour the liquid into it.
3. Top off with cola.

BRIGHT GREEN COOLER

3 measures pineapple juice
2 measures lime juice
1 measure green peppermint syrup
cracked ice cubes
ginger ale
cucumber strip and lime slice,
   to decorate

1. Shake the pineapple juice, lime juice, and green peppermint syrup vigorously over cracked ice until well frosted.
2. Fill a chilled highball glass halfway with cracked ice and strain the cocktail over it.
3. Top off with ginger ale and dress with the cucumber strip and lime slice.

COCONUT CREAM

1½ cups pineapple juice
⅓ cup coconut milk
⅔ cup vanilla ice cream
1 cup frozen pineapple chunks
2 scooped-out coconut shells,
   to serve (optional)
grated fresh coconut, to decorate

1. Pour the pineapple juice and coconut milk into a blender. Add the ice cream and process until smooth.
2. Add the pineapple chunks and process until smooth.
3. Divide the mixture between 2 scooped-out coconut shells, or tall glasses, and decorate with the grated fresh coconut.

UNDER THE BOARDWALK

crushed ice cubes
2 measures lemon juice
½ tsp sugar syrup
½ peach, peeled, pitted, and chopped
sparkling water
raspberries, to decorate

1. In a blender, process the crushed ice with the lemon juice, sugar syrup, and peach until slushy.
2. Pour into a chilled lowball glass.
3. Top off with sparkling water and stir gently. Dress with the raspberries.

FRUIT COOLER

1 cup orange juice
½ cup plain yogurt
2 eggs
2 bananas, peeled, sliced, and frozen
fresh banana slices, to decorate

1. Pour the orange juice and yogurt into a blender and process gently until combined.
2. Add the eggs and frozen bananas and process until smooth.
3. Pour the mixture into chilled highball glasses and dress with the fresh banana slices.

RANCH GIRL

SERVES 1

THIS DRINK IS PERFECT FOR A SUNDAY BRUNCH WHEN ALCOHOL MAY
BE TOO SOPORIFIC, BUT YOU WANT TO WAKE UP YOUR TASTE BUDS
AND SET THEM TINGLING.

1 measure lime juice
1 measure barbecue sauce
dash Worcestershire sauce
dash Tabasco sauce
cracked ice cubes
tomato juice
lime slices, to decorate

1. Shake the lime juice, barbecue sauce, Worcestershire sauce, and Tabasco sauce over cracked ice until well frosted.
2. Pour into a chilled highball glass, top off with tomato juice, and stir.
3. Dress with the lime slices.

New England Party

THIS IS A TAKE ON THE CLASSIC BLOODY MARY, WITHOUT THE ALCOHOL. CLAM JUICE IS AVAILABLE IN BOTTLED FORM IN SUPERMARKETS AND HAS A BRINY FLAVOR.

crushed ice cubes
dash Tabasco sauce
dash Worcestershire sauce
1 tsp lemon juice
1 carrot, chopped
4 celery stalks, 2 chopped and
   2 reserved whole to decorate
1¼ cups tomato juice
⅔ cup clam juice
salt and pepper

1. Put all the ingredients except the whole celery stalks into a blender and process until smooth.
2. Transfer to a pitcher, cover, and chill for about an hour.
3. Pour into 2 chilled highball glasses and season to taste with salt and pepper.
4. Dress with the reserved celery stalks.

Cocoberry

⅔ cup raspberries, plus extra to decorate
crushed ice cubes
1 measure coconut cream
⅔ cup pineapple juice
pineapple wedge, to decorate

1. Rub the raspberries through a metal strainer
   with the back of a spoon and transfer the
   puree to a blender.
2. Add the crushed ice, coconut cream, and
   pineapple juice. Blend until smooth, then pour
   the mixture, without straining, into a chilled
   lowball glass.
3. Dress with the pineapple wedge and
   raspberries.

Peachy Cream

2 measures peach juice, chilled
2 measures light cream
cracked ice cubes

1. Shake the peach juice and cream vigorously
   over cracked ice until well frosted.
2. Fill a chilled highball glass halfway with
   cracked ice and strain over the cocktail.

Traditional Lemonade

3 ripe lemons
generous ½ cup superfine sugar, or to taste
4 cups boiling water
cracked ice cubes
lemon slices, to decorate

1. Thinly pare the lemon rind.
2. Put the lemon rind into a heatproof bowl with the sugar. Pour over the boiling water and stir until the sugar has dissolved. Cover and let cool.
3. Squeeze out the juice from the lemons and pour into the cooled syrup. Strain into a pitcher. Taste and add more sugar if needed.
4. Fill 4 highball glasses with cracked ice, pour in the lemonade, and dress with the lemon slices.

Raspberry Lemonade

2 lemons
1 cup confectioners' sugar
¾ cup raspberries
few drops vanilla extract
cracked ice cubes
sparkling water
fresh mint sprigs,
   to decorate

1. Halve the lemons, scoop out and chop the flesh, and place in a blender with the sugar, raspberries, vanilla extract, and cracked ice. Blend for 2–3 minutes.
2. Fill 4 highball glasses with cracked ice, strain in the lemonade, and top off with sparkling water.
3. Dress with the mint sprigs.

Cucumber Refresher

SERVES I

THIS COOLING, THIRST-QUENCHING COCKTAIL IS GREAT TO SERVE
AT A SUMMER PARTY—THE CUCUMBER INSIDE THE GLASS WILL BE A
REAL TALKING POINT!

2–3 fresh mint sprigs
1 tsp confectioners' sugar
juice 1 lime
1-inch/2.5-cm piece cucumber,
   thinly sliced
cracked ice cubes
sparkling water, chilled

1. Remove the leaves from the mint
sprigs and chop finely. Mix half of
the chopped mint with the sugar
on a saucer.

2. Rub a little of the lime juice
around the rim of a wine glass and
dip in the minted sugar to frost.

3. Put the remaining lime juice and
chopped mint into the prepared
glass with the cucumber and
cracked ice. Top off with chilled
sparkling water.

Orange & Lime Iced Tea

Serves 2

Iced tea is always refreshing and, even if you are not a tea drinker, this version is especially fresh and fruity. Keep some in the refrigerator if you don't use it all up.

1¼ cups boiling water
2 tea bags
scant ½ cup orange juice
4 tbsp lime juice
1–2 tbsp brown sugar
lime wedge
granulated sugar
cracked ice cubes

1. Pour the boiling water into a heatproof pitcher, add the tea bags, and let stand for 5 minutes. Remove the tea bags and let the tea cool, then chill.
2. When chilled, pour in the orange juice and lime juice. Add the brown sugar to taste and stir.
3. Rub the rims of 2 lowball glasses with the lime wedge, then dip into the granulated sugar. Fill the prepared glasses with cracked ice, then pour in the tea.

SUNRISE

SERVES 1

cracked ice cubes
2 measures orange juice
1 measure lemon juice
1 measure grenadine
sparkling water

1. Put the cracked ice into a chilled highball glass and pour the orange juice, lemon juice, and grenadine over it.
2. Stir together well and top off with sparkling water.

BANANA COFFEE BREAK

SERVES 2

1¼ cups milk
4 tbsp instant coffee powder
⅔ cup vanilla ice cream
2 bananas, peeled, sliced, and frozen
brown sugar

1. Pour the milk into a blender, add the coffee powder, and process gently until combined.
2. Add half the ice cream and process gently, then add the remaining ice cream and process until well combined. When the mixture is thoroughly blended, add the bananas and sugar to taste and process until smooth.
3. Pour into 2 chilled highball glasses.

Juicy Julep

SERVES 1

1 measure orange juice
1 measure pineapple juice
1 measure lime juice
½ measure raspberry syrup
cracked ice cubes
4 crushed fresh mint leaves,
   plus an extra sprig to garnish
ginger ale

1. Shake the orange juice, pineapple juice, lime juice, and raspberry syrup vigorously over cracked ice with the crushed mint leaves until well frosted.
2. Strain into a chilled highball glass, top off with ginger ale, and stir gently.
3. Dress with the mint sprig.

Eye of the Hurricane

SERVES 1

2 measures passion fruit syrup
1 measure lime juice
cracked ice cubes
bitter lemon
lemon slice, to decorate

1. Pour the passion fruit syrup and lime juice over cracked ice in a mixing glass.
2. Stir well to mix and strain into a chilled tumbler.
3. Top off with bitter lemon and dress with the lemon slice.